The Homeless

OPPOSING VIEWPOINTS ®

Other Books of Related Interest

OPPOSING VIEWPOINTS SERIES

Addiction
Alcohol
America's Prisons
Chemical Dependency
Civil Liberties
Domestic Violence
Drug Abuse
The Family
Health Care
Human Rights
Mental Illness
Poverty
Violence
Welfare

CURRENT CONTROVERSIES SERIES

Alcoholism
Family Violence
Mental Health
Violence Against Women

AT ISSUE SERIES

Domestic Violence
Single-Parent Families
Welfare Reform

The
Homeless

O P P O S I N G   V I E W P O I N T S ®

Jennifer A. Hurley, *Book Editor*

Bonnie Szumski, *Editorial Director*
Scott Barbour, *Managing Editor*

OPPOSING
VIEWPOINTS®
SERIES

Greenhaven Press, Inc., San Diego, California

Cover photo: © Digital Stock

Library of Congress Cataloging-in-Publication Data

The homeless / Jennifer A. Hurley, book editor.
    p. cm. — (Opposing viewpoints series)
    Includes bibliographical references and index.
    ISBN 0-7377-0749-6 (pbk. : alk. paper) —
ISBN 0-7377-0750-X (lib. : alk. paper)
    1. Homelessness. I. Hurley, Jennifer A., 1973–   II. Series

HV4493 .H644 2002
362.5—dc21   2001023916
                                                           CIP

Greenhaven Press, Inc., P.O. Box 289009
San Diego, CA 92198-9009

"Congress shall make
no law...abridging the
freedom of speech, or of
the press."

First Amendment to the U.S. Constitution

The basic foundation of our democracy is the First
Amendment guarantee of freedom of expression.
The Opposing Viewpoints Series is dedicated to the
concept of this basic freedom and the idea that it is
more important to practice it than to enshrine it.

Contents

Why Consider Opposing Viewpoints?   9

Introduction   12

Chapter 1: Is Homelessness a Serious Problem?

Chapter Preface   16

1. Homelessness Is a Serious Problem for Society   17
   Washington Spectator

2. Homelessness Is Not Society's Problem   23
   C.J. Carnacchio

3. Homelessness Is a Problem in Cities   28
   America

4. Homelessness Is a Problem in Rural Communities   33
   Yvonne M. Vissing

5. Homelessness Is a Problem Among Women and
   Children   39
   Eugene M. Lewit and Linda Schuurmann Baker

6. Homelessness Is a Serious Problem Among Men   45
   Anthony Browne

Periodical Bibliography   51

**Chapter 2: What Are the Causes of
Homelessness?**

Chapter Preface   53

1. Low Wages and Limited Employment
   Opportunities Cause Homelessness   54
   Aimee Molloy

2. Homelessness Is Often Voluntary   59
   Bob Klug

3. Lack of Affordable Housing Causes Homelessness   63
   Bruce Burleson

4. Welfare Cuts Have Increased Homelessness   68
   Leslie Miller

5. Mental Illness Contributes to Homelessness   72
   Henry G. Cisneros

6. Substance Abuse Is a Cause of Homelessness   78
   San Diego Regional Task Force on the Homeless

7. Domestic Violence Contributes to Homelessness   84
   National Coalition for the Homeless

Periodical Bibliography   88

Chapter 3: What Housing Options Would Benefit the Homeless?

Chapter Preface   90

1. The Federal Government Should Work to Provide
   Affordable Housing   91
   Andrew Cuomo

2. The Federal Government Should Not Work to
   Provide Affordable Housing   99
   Howard Husock

3. Housing Vouchers Benefit Low-Income Families   111
   Merrill Matthews Jr.

4. Housing Vouchers Do Not Always Benefit
   Low-Income Families   117
   Ann O'Hanlon

5. SROs Offer a Solution to Homelessness   125
   The Economist

6. SROs Are Currently an Inadequate Solution to
   Homelessness   129
   *British Columbia Ministry of Social Development
   and Economic Security*

Periodical Bibliography   134

Chapter 4: How Should Society Deal with the Homeless?

Chapter Preface   136

1. The Hardcore Homeless Should Be Arrested   137
   David Brooks

2. Society Should Not Criminalize the Homeless   142
   Karl Lydersen

3. Some of the Homeless Mentally Ill Should Be
   Treated Involuntarily   150
   E. Fuller Torrey

4. The Homeless Mentally Ill Should Not Be Treated
   Involuntarily   155
   Chance Martin

5. Private Charities Can Help the Homeless   159
   Michael Tanner

6. Private Charities Cannot Help All of the Homeless   163
   Joseph P. Shapiro and Jennifer Seter

Periodical Bibliography   168

For Further Discussion   169
Organizations and Websites   171
Bibliography of Books   177
Index   180

Why Consider Opposing Viewpoints?

"The only way in which a human being can make some approach to knowing the whole of a subject is by hearing what can be said about it by persons of every variety of opinion and studying all modes in which it can be looked at by every character of mind. No wise man ever acquired his wisdom in any mode but this."

John Stuart Mill

In our media-intensive culture it is not difficult to find differing opinions. Thousands of newspapers and magazines and dozens of radio and television talk shows resound with differing points of view. The difficulty lies in deciding which opinion to agree with and which "experts" seem the most credible. The more inundated we become with differing opinions and claims, the more essential it is to hone critical reading and thinking skills to evaluate these ideas. Opposing Viewpoints books address this problem directly by presenting stimulating debates that can be used to enhance and teach these skills. The varied opinions contained in each book examine many different aspects of a single issue. While examining these conveniently edited opposing views, readers can develop critical thinking skills such as the ability to compare and contrast authors' credibility, facts, argumentation styles, use of persuasive techniques, and other stylistic tools. In short, the Opposing Viewpoints Series is an ideal way to attain the higher-level thinking and reading skills so essential in a culture of diverse and contradictory opinions.

In addition to providing a tool for critical thinking, Opposing Viewpoints books challenge readers to question their own strongly held opinions and assumptions. Most people form their opinions on the basis of upbringing, peer pressure, and personal, cultural, or professional bias. By reading carefully balanced opposing views, readers must directly confront new ideas as well as the opinions of those with whom they disagree. This is not to simplistically argue that everyone who reads opposing views will—or should—change his or her opinion. Instead, the series enhances readers' understanding of their own views by encouraging confrontation with opposing ideas. Careful examination of others' views can lead to the readers' understanding of the logical inconsistencies in their own opinions, perspective on why they hold an opinion, and the consideration of the possibility that their opinion requires further evaluation.

Evaluating Other Opinions

To ensure that this type of examination occurs, Opposing Viewpoints books present all types of opinions. Prominent spokespeople on different sides of each issue as well as well-known professionals from many disciplines challenge the reader. An additional goal of the series is to provide a forum for other, less known, or even unpopular viewpoints. The opinion of an ordinary person who has had to make the decision to cut off life support from a terminally ill relative, for example, may be just as valuable and provide just as much insight as a medical ethicist's professional opinion. The editors have two additional purposes in including these less known views. One, the editors encourage readers to respect others' opinions—even when not enhanced by professional credibility. It is only by reading or listening to and objectively evaluating others' ideas that one can determine whether they are worthy of consideration. Two, the inclusion of such viewpoints encourages the important critical thinking skill of objectively evaluating an author's credentials and bias. This evaluation will illuminate an author's reasons for taking a particular stance on an issue and will aid in readers' evaluation of the author's ideas.

It is our hope that these books will give readers a deeper understanding of the issues debated and an appreciation of the complexity of even seemingly simple issues when good and honest people disagree. This awareness is particularly important in a democratic society such as ours in which people enter into public debate to determine the common good. Those with whom one disagrees should not be regarded as enemies but rather as people whose views deserve careful examination and may shed light on one's own.

Thomas Jefferson once said that "difference of opinion leads to inquiry, and inquiry to truth." Jefferson, a broadly educated man, argued that "if a nation expects to be ignorant and free . . . it expects what never was and never will be." As individuals and as a nation, it is imperative that we consider the opinions of others and examine them with skill and discernment. The Opposing Viewpoints Series is intended to help readers achieve this goal.

David L. Bender and Bruno Leone,
Founders

Greenhaven Press anthologies primarily consist of previously published material taken from a variety of sources, including periodicals, books, scholarly journals, newspapers, government documents, and position papers from private and public organizations. These original sources are often edited for length and to ensure their accessibility for a young adult audience. The anthology editors also change the original titles of these works in order to clearly present the main thesis of each viewpoint and to explicitly indicate the opinion presented in the viewpoint. These alterations are made in consideration of both the reading and comprehension levels of a young adult audience. Every effort is made to ensure that Greenhaven Press accurately reflects the original intent of the authors included in this anthology.

Introduction

"[Criminalizing homeless people] isn't only inhumane and potentially unconstitutional, but it's also senseless and ineffective."
　　　　　　—*Maria Foscarinis*, Christian Science Monitor,
　　　　　　　　　　　　　　　　　　December 9, 1999

"Experience tells us strong enforcement against quality-of-life crimes makes [cities] safer in every way."
　　—*Richard Riordan*, Los Angeles Times, *January 29, 1997*

In Orlando, Florida, being homeless is becoming increasing difficult. Since February 1997, anyone wishing to panhandle on the streets must wear a laminated panhandling permit issued by the police department. Homeless people who hold permits are restricted from panhandling in certain areas—including bus depots, train stations, public parks, and sports arenas—and must follow a lengthy set of guidelines. They cannot, as commentator Eric Brosch writes,

> approach people at ATMs or in vehicles, or come within three feet of the person solicited. They can't use obscenities, follow people, or work in pairs. Panhandlers may not make false representations, which include: stating that the donation is required for a need that does not exist or that the solicitor is from out of town and stranded when it is not true, wearing a military uniform without having served, pretending to be disabled or using "any make-up or device to simulate any deformity." Furthermore, it is illegal to beg "for a specific purpose and then spend the funds received for a different purpose."

Homeless people who panhandle without an official permit, or who break any of the rules, may be required to pay fines of up to $500—a stiff penalty for someone whose source of income is panhandling—or can be arrested and may spend up to 60 days in jail.

Orlando is just one of many cities that are applying legal sanctions to homeless people who live on the streets. New York City mayor Rudy Giuliani began the effort in the mid-1990s with "quality-of-life" ordinances that forbid the homeless from sleeping in public parks and ticket what he calls "squeegee terrorists" who wash car windows in hopes of receiving a handout. In 1999, after a homeless man injured a woman by slamming her head with a brick, Giuliani ordered that homeless people who refused city-provided shelter would face arrest. Under the mayor's new policy, homeless people must work for their shelter; if the head of a homeless family will not work, the family's children may be sent to foster care.

Other cities following Giuliani's approach include Chicago, where policymakers recently erected giant chain-link fences around a downtown area to prevent vagrants from loitering there, and Cleveland, where homeless people sleeping on the sidewalks are subject to arrest. Even San Francisco, considered to be one of the most tolerant cities in the nation, now bans homeless people from camping in parks or sleeping in doorways, arrests people who give food to the homeless without a permit, and recently considered a proposal to confiscate homeless people's shopping carts.

Some contend that local governments' attempts to crack down on the homeless reflect the widespread view that, in today's booming economy, homelessness is the result of laziness. Paul Boden, director of the San Francisco Coalition on Homelessness, says that "there is an attitude that with unemployment at record lows, with the stock market at record highs, if you're poor, it's your own damn fault." As a result, claim *U.S. News & World Report* writers Warren Cohen and Mike Tharp, the public has little tolerance for homelessness. "[I]nstead of sympathy," they write, "street dwellers are attracting hostility. Residents are sick of being hassled by ever more aggressive cadgers, and vendors say mendicants are hurting business."

Proponents of measures to crack down on homelessness argue that the homeless are a public nuisance whose presence on the streets harms businesses, impedes the rehabilitation of dilapidated urban areas, and makes life unpleasant—or even dangerous—for other citizens. Furthermore, city officials contend, the new ordinances force homeless individuals to seek the assistance they need—be it alcohol or drug treatment, mental health care, or employment services.

Advocates for the homeless, on the other hand, argue that such laws rob homeless people of their civil rights and their dignity. As stated by the *Safety Network*, a publication of the National Coalition for the Homeless,

> These city ordinances . . . are misguided because they seek to hide homeless people, not to end homelessness. They are unjust because they seek to punish people for being poor. They are, in effect, persecution because people who are homeless do not have the option to rest, sleep, and set down belongings in private. People who are forced to live on the streets have very few choices: Are these cities asking people who are homeless to choose *not to exist!*?

Moreover, maintain critics, city ordinances that target the homeless are a waste of resources. Carol Sobel, an attorney with the Southern California branch of the American Civil Liberties Union, asks, "What is it you want your police to be doing? We don't have enough people working on homicides. . . . Do we want to shift the limited resources that we have to arresting somebody who washes somebody's window without permission?" Sobel and other opponents of the new laws argue that instead of wasting money trying to "hide" the homeless, the government should use its economic resources to address the causes of homelessness, such as low wages and lack of affordable housing.

With the numbers of homeless rising despite widespread prosperity—a 2000 study by the Urban Institute reports that as many as 3.5 million people are homeless, compared to 1.8 million in 1987—the problem of homelessness is once again in the public limelight. In *The Homeless: Opposing Viewpoints*, various commentators, including people who have experienced homelessness themselves, examine the causes of homelessness and offer proposals for reducing the problem. Chapters address the following questions: Is Homelessness a Serious Problem? What Are the Causes of Homelessness? What Housing Options Would Benefit the Homeless? and How Should Society Deal with the Homeless? Throughout these chapters, authors debate the plight of those who live in the shadowy margins of society.

CHAPTER 1

Is Homelessness a Serious Problem?

Chapter Preface

How many people in the United States are homeless? Because statistics documenting the extent of homelessness vary widely, there is no easy answer to this question. For example, the National Coalition for the Homeless and the Urban Institute estimate that on an average night there are over 700,000 people sleeping on the streets or in homeless shelters. Other organizations, however, argue that this number is exaggerated, and that in truth only 300,000 people are homeless on any given night.

The difficulty in determining the number of homeless people in the United States is caused in part by disparities in the definition of homelessness. Some experts in the field assert that there are two broad categories of homelessness, which sometimes overlap. The first category, episodic homelessness, refers to people who are temporarily homeless because of extreme poverty. Homeless people in this category often experience problems such as a lack of job prospects or domestic violence; however, according to the Department of Health and Human Services, "their persistent poverty is the decisive factor that turns unforeseen crises, or even minor setbacks, into bouts of homelessness." Oftentimes, the episodically homeless are only homeless for brief periods of time.

The chronically homeless, who comprise the second category, are those for whom homelessness has become a way of life. Like the episodic homeless, they lack financial resources; however, because their homelessness generally stems from severe mental illness, alcohol or drug addiction, or persistent health problems, they are less likely to regain a stable living situation.

Some commentators argue that because the episodically homeless are usually undercounted by statisticians, the problem of homelessness is more serious than the numbers indicate. Other analysts maintain that episodic homelessness is not a grave problem, since many who fall into this category eventually escape homelessness. The following chapter offers conflicting opinions on the seriousness of homelessness in America.

"Lack of jobs, lack of income, lack of housing, drug addiction, mental illness, and now lack of welfare and social services contribute to the misery and homelessness of approximately 730,000 people in the U.S. on a given day."

Homelessness Is a Serious Problem for Society

Washington Spectator

Although homelessness has largely faded from the public's consciousness, the problem continues to worsen, argues the *Washington Spectator* in the following viewpoint. Lack of adequate-paying jobs, affordable housing, welfare, and services for the mentally ill have left society's poorest members with no place to go. The *Washington Spectator* is a semimonthly publication of the Public Concern Foundation, a nonprofit organization that champions progressive values.

As you read, consider the following questions:
1. What attitude do most Americans take toward the homeless, according to the author?
2. As stated by the author, what evidence exists that the poor live in substandard housing?
3. How many people seek homeless shelter in an average winter month, according to the *Washington Spectator*?

Excerpted from "America's Poorest People Have No Place to Go," editorial, *The Washington Spectator*, February 1, 2000. Reprinted with permission. For subscriptions write to: *The Washington Spectator*, PO Box 20065, London Terrace Station, New York, NY 10011 or call (212) 741-2365.

A journalistically superb photographic display called "The Way Home—Ending Homelessness in America" has just closed at the Corcoran Gallery of Art, Washington's oldest art museum, and will be on tour elsewhere in coming months. It includes 150 starkly candid pictures of homeless men, women and children, adrift in doorways, on streets and in alleys.

One photo shows two limousine chauffeurs ignoring a homeless man, asleep on the sidewalk nearby, while they chat in the dark and wait for their passengers to finish dinner in a restaurant. Their indifference is grimly symbolic.

The pictures were taken by well-known photographers, including Tipper Gore, who is less known as a photographer and a homeless activist than as the wife of Vice President Al Gore.

It is Mrs. Gore, who was once a photographer on the staff of the *Nashville Tennessean* when her husband was a reporter there, who has given both the photo display and the widely unrecognized saga of the growing number of homeless people in America a badly needed shot of attention. She has nine stunning photographs in the exhibit, and she has done a vigorous public-relations job in waking up the country to the plight of our prosperity's less fortunate. . . .

But the homeless have only moved slowly toward getting public attention. Homelessness has faded from public consciousness. Although the plight of the homeless received some recent national press attention following the sweep-them-off-the-streets cruelties in New York and San Francisco and the random shootings of the homeless in Denver, the full scope of what is a national humanitarian disgrace has largely been ignored by the media.

The Stigma

The homeless are also ignored by the growing number of Americans who are beneficiaries of the booming economy, and who tend to view drifters on the street with disgust or indifference. The attitude seems to be that if they are that poor it's their fault, and more and more cities are shooing the homeless out of sight. The police in 24 cities that are fed up with the homeless conduct nightly "sweeps" of loiterers, beggars and street sleepers.

An ironic editorial-page cartoon in the *Boston Globe* showed two well-dressed, briefcase-toting executives walking by a bearded homeless man, stretched out for a nap on a park bench. As the strollers pass him by, the homeless man is wrapped for warmth in a fully opened newspaper displaying the large-type headlines: "Economy Soars" and "Shelters Full." Without looking at the homeless man, one passing fat-cat remarks to the other, "Nowadays, everyone has a home page."

Little noticed, some help is on the way. In what the White House called a Christmas gift to the homeless, President Clinton announced on Christmas day [1999] that he was assigning $900 million in grants to make homeless-shelter improvements, and improve housing, job training and health and drug addiction programs for the homeless. But Washington is no Santa Claus. To paraphrase a Ronald Reagan slogan of the 1980s, for the homeless it is still *mourning* in America. Major trends in recent decades have worsened their plight.

It's Worse than the Depression

Lack of jobs, lack of income, lack of housing, drug addiction, mental illness, and now lack of welfare and social services contribute to the misery and homelessness of approximately 730,000 people in the U.S. on a given day—a total number that goes as high as 2 million during a year.

In the late 1960s and through the 1970s, the massive destruction of marginal, low-rent housing by urban renewal programs took away affordable family and single-occupancy homes from many poverty-level Americans. Decaying urban neighborhoods were razed. For many, the new housing that replaced the old is not affordable.

During the same period, declining federal and state financial support for mental hospitals and outpatient programs, and the belief that medications could make the hospitalized mentally ill self-reliant, forced many patients onto the streets where they languish, abandoned and unsupervised. Some are psychically damaged veterans of the war in Vietnam. The deinstitutionalizing of the mentally disabled, who have been left without community services and places to seek help, is now seen as a major cause of homelessness.

The Widening Gap Between the Rich and the Poor

More recently, experts on homelessness believe that the widening gap between the well-off and the impoverished, complicated for many by the ending of welfare and by enforced work at the minimum-wage level, has compounded the problem. According to Cushing Dolbeare, a veteran pioneer in homeless care, who founded the National Low Income Housing Council in Washington, "In this, the best-housed nation in the world in most respects, the problem of housing affordability is pervasive." Her studies show that while many households must spend more than half their total income on rent, they are living in seriously substandard housing.

A recent report by the Department of Housing and Urban Development (HUD) confirms that a steep decline in housing subsidies has left 5.3 million poor families, a record number, in housing that is substandard and possibly unaffordable.

From 1975 to 1998 the proportion of the national income received by the poorest one-fifth of Americans dropped from 4.4 to 3.6 percent. The proportion going to the wealthiest fifth climbed from 43 percent to 49 percent. HUD has placed the average monthly income of the homeless at $267.

The income of some homeless families is so low that they cannot pay electricity and water bills, even if they can afford what is called a fair-market rent. In the 10 least-affordable metropolitan areas across the country, more than half the low-income families cannot afford a two-bedroom apartment, according to the National Low Income Housing Coalition. In the 10 worst rural areas, that percentage is as high as 80 percent, and unpaid rent and utility bills bring evictions.

According to Nan Roman, the president of the Washington-based, non-profit National Alliance to End Homelessness, during a single year in New York City and Philadelphia one in ten poor children, and one in six African-American children, experiences homelessness for some period of time.

Roman and others believe that the homelessness now being experienced by so many is different from the family dislocations and skid row experiences of the Great Depression, the historic image of hardship lodged in the minds of generations of Americans. And it is experienced differently by the homeless. These experts agree that the one generality of homelessness today is the critical shortage of affordable housing, leaving as many as 5 million households in need of better, safer and more secure homes, and many thousands on the street.

"SORRY... I'M SUFFERING FROM COMPASSION FATIGUE."

Jim Borgman. Reprinted by special permission of King Features Syndicate.

There is now a sweeping new survey of the homeless, spurred largely by the Secretary of Housing and Urban Development, Andrew Cuomo, who is also chairman of the Interagency Council on Homelessness, which involves 12 federal agencies. When the survey findings were published by HUD in early December, they got only spotty press attention. The *New York Times* gave the data released in "The Forgotten Americans," the 600-page government report on the homeless, lengthy coverage (December 5 and 8, 1999). The findings of the most comprehensive study of the homeless ever done were newsworthy, if ugly, but we saw little mention of them elsewhere.

There is still no final national estimate of the total number of the homeless, but according to the HUD study, during an average winter month some 470,000 men, women and children seek and receive homeless shelter, if only for days or weeks. Twenty percent of the children living with homeless parents are infants or toddlers, 33 percent are of elementary school age, and 20 percent are adolescents.

The number in transit—those who move from shelter to shelter, from briefly held jobs that allow them temporarily to afford their own housing, or from city to city—are 25 percent of the total number of homeless during a given year. Overall, many are deeply impoverished and many are ill.

Not even counting those with AIDS, two-thirds of the homeless suffer from chronic or infectious diseases, and 39 percent show signs of drug or alcohol addiction and/or mental illness. Yet 55 percent have no health insurance, and in the HUD survey 24 percent said they had needed medical attention in the past year but were unable to get it.

Forty percent of the homeless are in families, mostly women with children, and the rest are single, mostly men. Forty percent of those surveyed had gone without food for one or more days in the previous month. Almost one-third said they had slept on the streets, in parks, in church entrances or other public places within the week before they were interviewed.

> *"Liberals and homeless advocates have succeeded in manufacturing [the] so-called [homeless] crisis not only by exaggerating numbers but also by distorting the truth about the roots of homelessness."*

Homelessness Is Not Society's Problem

C.J. Carnacchio

In the following viewpoint, C.J. Carnacchio contends that homeless advocates have exaggerated the scope and severity of homelessness. In truth, he writes, the group of homeless people who are victims of forces beyond their control is extremely small. Most homeless people become homeless because they are unwilling to assume the responsibilities of maintaining a job and a permanent residence. Homelessness is caused by a lack of personal responsibility, argues Carnacchio, and therefore should not be considered society's problem to solve.

As you read, consider the following questions:

1. How many people in the United States are homeless, according to the author?
2. In Carnacchio's opinion, what facts about the homeless do homeless advocates ignore?
3. What should be done with the mentally ill homeless, in the author's view?

Excerpted from "Homeless Advocates Must Face Facts," by C.J. Carnacchio, *Michigan Review*, November 19, 1997. Reprinted with permission.

Back in the 1980s, homeless advocates were often fond of telling their media lapdogs that there were anywhere from two to three million homeless in the United States. However, both the Urban Institute and the U.S. Census Bureau estimate the number of homeless to be in the neighborhood of 300,000 to 600,000. Despite this hard evidence, many Americans still believe that there are millions of homeless and consequently that there is a "homeless crisis" in the U.S.

Liberals and homeless advocates have succeeded in manufacturing this so-called crisis not only by exaggerating numbers but also by distorting the truth about the roots of homelessness. The media has served as an all-too-willing accomplice in the advocates' Machiavellian charade. In his book *Rude Awakenings*, Richard W. White Jr. points out that "homelessness became a crisis to most Americans after the media introduced the term and labeled it a crisis. Before then it was not a crisis or even a problem." Reporters never questioned the statistic or the claims of the homeless advocacy's propaganda.

Both advocates and the media portray the homeless as simply ordinary Americans down on their luck, victims of cruel economic forces and a housing crisis. They delight in telling us that we are all just one paycheck away from living on the streets. But the pure down-on-their-luck group is relatively small—about 15 percent. They are highly visible in media stories about the homeless because advocates learned long ago that this group elicits the most support for their cause.

Ignored is the substance abuse, criminal behavior, and mental illness which characterizes the majority of the homeless. Advocates and the media neglect to tell us that seven out of ten homeless have been institutionalized at one time or another; this includes mental hospitals, detoxification centers, and prison.

Advocates and the media always argue that it is external forces, not individual choices, that lead to homelessness. Personal responsibility is never an issue. They place the blame on faceless corporations, evil Republicans, and a selfish society.

Consequently, many homeless have become offensive and even violent in their behavior as they have come to believe that everyone who passes them owes them something. They used to believe that their plight was their own fault but, as White observes, "Now, because of what they [homeless] hear in protest songs, read in newspapers, see on television, hear from advocates, or learn from the social system, they think that their condition is someone else's fault. Some act as if they are morally superior to people who work and raise a family." But, the fact is that in the majority of cases, the homeless are either directly responsible for their plight or some individual-based problem is at work.

Not Willing to Assume Responsibilities

Advocates refuse to acknowledge that there is a certain percentage of homeless who CHOOSE to live that way. They are not willing to assume the responsibilities associated with maintaining a job and a permanent residence. They prefer the mythical "freedom" of the streets and turn down shelter even when it's offered to them.

Breaking Down Barriers to Affordable Housing

Strides have been made in breaking down what many housing experts of the 1990s suggested were the barriers to an adequate supply of low-cost housing and thus one major cause of homelessness. There have been both advances in modular home construction techniques and increased flexibility integrated into building and zoning standards around the country, making modular housing a viable and lower cost alternative to stick-built dwellings. Recent court rulings have decreased exclusionary practices, like large lot zoning, which previously characterized many suburban fringe areas and which housing experts argued drove up housing costs. New building codes and the relaxation of multiple occupancy restrictions have contributed.

Ralph S. Hambrick Jr. and Gary T. Johnson, *Society*, September/ October 1998.

Next, current estimates indicate that roughly a third or more of the homeless are drug addicts or alcoholics. Homeless advocates argue that substance abuse is a result, not a cause, of homelessness. They reason that such substances are used by the homeless to escape the reality of their wretched lives, thereby absolving them of any responsibility or blame.

But, as White points out, "In Los Angeles' inner city, Paul Koegel and M. Audrey Burnam found that nearly 80 percent of alcoholics in their sample of homeless adults 'reported that their first alcoholic symptom occurred before they were first homeless' and that in 57 percent of the cases this occurred at least five years before their first episode of homelessness."

Alcoholism and drug abuse are the result of individual choices such as a willingness to sacrifice career, family, and health in favor of getting high. Human beings are capable of both good and bad decisions, but no matter which road is taken, responsibility must always be assigned to the individual choice-maker.

Many homeless advocates have failed to see that their aid programs have in fact perpetuated substance abuse. As Dr. E. Fuller Torrey, a clinical and research psychiatrist, points out, "When one is addicted to alcohol or drugs, the highest priority is to save as much money as possible to feed that addiction. Present homeless policies, which in some cities have guaranteed free beds and food for everyone who asks, have probably exacerbated rather than relieved the problem of homeless substance abuse." These free services, coupled with the homeless' panhandling incomes (and in some cases welfare benefits), allow them to fund their self-destructive habits and perpetuate a cycle of dependency.

Homeless Criminals

The frequency of criminal behavior is another aspect of the homeless population advocates fail to mention. In his book *Without Shelter: Homelessness in the 1980s*, Peter H. Rossi found that 42 percent of the homeless, catalogued in 16 studies, spent some amount of time in jail or prison. Again, advocates argue that desperation forces the homeless into criminal activity. But a 1986 study conducted by the National Bureau of Economic Research found that 61 percent of homeless' jail time occurred before their homelessness and even "suggested that [unsuccessful] crime leads to homelessness."

Experts also estimate that another third of the homeless suffer from severe mental illness. While clearly this is not the result of bad individual choices, it is still a problem confined to the individual and not in any way society's fault. Advocates argue that it is the stress of homeless life which causes these mental problems. But in the book *Homelessness, Health, and Human Needs*, the Institute of Medicine found that severe mental illnesses "are unlikely to result from the trauma of homelessness." In fact, few psychiatrists still subscribe to the notion that mental illnesses such as schizophrenia can happen to anyone given the right environmental conditions. . . .

The mentally ill homeless should either be institutionalized, put into the care of family members or legal guardians, or forced, as a condition of being allowed into society, to take the necessary medications to control their illness. Many of the homeless could function in society if only they took their medication. But groups like the American Civil Liberties Union will not allow these measures because they would infringe upon the homeless' civil rights.

But, as psychiatrist/columnist Charles Krauthammer retorted, "For the severely mentally ill, however, liberty is not just an empty word but a cruel hoax. Free to do what? What does freedom mean for a paranoid schizophrenic who is ruled by voices commanded by his persecutors and rattling around in his head?" The ACLU is more interested in defending their right to sleep in parks and bus terminals than actually salvaging their lives. It is precisely this kind of feeble thinking that has led to the idiocy of the "homeless rights" movement. . . .

All things considered, the Left has no real interest in an honest and frank discussion about the true roots of homelessness or the role of personal responsibility. Why should they? The homeless provide them with living political symbols of what they claim is the failure and injustice of capitalism coupled with the cruelty of the wealthy. They are paraded before the media as victims of evil Republican policies. Such images fuel feelings of guilt in many voters who consider themselves well-off by comparison. This guilt translates into calls for increased State action which in turn generates a larger electoral base for the Democrats and further growth of the behemoth State. By all accounts it is to the Left's advantage that the homeless stay homeless. Compassion indeed.

> *"The U.S. Conference of Mayors' annual 'Status Report on Hunger and Homelessness in American Cities'. . . reports that in the past year emergency shelter requests were up 15 percent for families."*

Homelessness Is a Problem in Cities

America

America, a national Catholic weekly magazine, states in the subsequent viewpoint that homelessness is worsening in U.S. cities. According to the author, the strong economy has led to dramatic rent increases in most major cities, forcing many poor families into homelessness. Moreover, homeless shelters and other forms of public housing cannot accommodate the growing number of homeless people in urban areas.

As you read, consider the following questions:

1. How many people are turned away from shelters for lack of resources, according to the author?
2. What percentage of shelter residents are employed, as reported by the author?
3. As cited by *America*, what are the five cities with the "meanest streets"?

D espite unprecedented prosperity, thousands of Americans are hungry and have no place to sleep at night. The U.S. Conference of Mayors' annual "Status Report on Hunger and Homelessness in American Cities," released in mid-December 1998, reports that in the past year emergency shelter requests were up 15 percent for families (11 percent overall), and requests for food assistance rose 14 percent.

Many of these homeless people are parents and their children. Children, in fact, make up a quarter of the homeless population. A number of studies have shown that the instability of their lives can lead to poor health, developmental delays and greater risks for anxiety and depression. Especially disturbing is the fact that requests for shelter and food cannot always be met; nearly a third of the families seeking shelter are turned away for lack of resources. In San Antonio, Tex., for example, families who can find no space in shelters sleep under bridges, in parks or in cars. Much the same bleak scenario holds true for food requests; because of the increased demand, emergency food agencies have frequently had to cut back both on the amounts distributed and on the number of times a month requests can be honored.

"Not Lifting All Boats"

Twenty percent of those in shelters are employed either full or part-time. One of the painful ironies of the situation is that in a number of cities—such as Denver, Boston and Philadelphia—the strong economy has led landlords to raise rents. As a result, parents employed in low-wage jobs are unable to pay for rent, food and other necessities and therefore end up in shelters, not infrequently separated from their children. As Philadelphia officials put it with considerable understatement, "the rising economic tide is not lifting all boats." The survey blames welfare reform to some degree for its negative effect on both hunger and homelessness. People who have lost their welfare benefits have not always found jobs with salaries sufficient to cover living costs; and often they do not realize that they may still be eligible for food stamps and so do not apply for them. The mayors' report, however, considers the main causes of the increase in shelter populations and emergency food requests to be jobs that pay too little and the lack of affordable housing. Other causes include substance abuse and mental health problems that go unaddressed because of a lack of needed services like case management, housing and treatment.

Increase in Demand for Emergency Food and Shelter

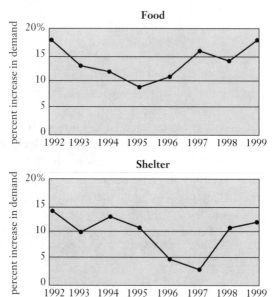

In spite of a strong economy and decreasing unemployment rates, an increasing number of people are requesting emergency food and shelter in the nation's cities, according to the U.S. Conference of Mayors. The organization attributes the increase to rising housing costs, as more prosperous citizens become more prevalent in urban neighborhoods.

Source: U.S. Conference of Mayors

As if the difficulties of homeless people were not bad enough, another recent report—released in early January 1999 by the National Law Center on Homelessness & Poverty in Washington, D.C.—describes local governments' continuing efforts to enact stringent anti-homeless legislation. The report, entitled "Out of Sight—Out of Mind?", documents the increasing criminalization of homeless men and women. The very title tells much of the story; many local governments try to remove homeless people from the public eye as bad for business. This has been particularly true of New York City, with its large concentrations of homeless persons. There the mayor's emphasis on so-called quality of life crimes has meant that homeless men and women have increasingly been pushed from affluent sections of Manhattan into the poorer surrounding boroughs. Sweeps, the report states, "continue on almost a nightly basis."

The "Meanest Streets"

Not surprisingly, the National Law Center's survey cites New York as one of five U.S. cities having the "meanest streets." The other four are Atlanta, Chicago, San Francisco and Tucson. But the center's report also gives credit to several cities whose officials are taking more constructive approaches. Dallas, for instance, provides birth certificates to homeless people, even to those from out of state, as a way of assisting them to apply for public housing. Public housing applicants around the nation, though, face waiting lists that average two years in length. The waiting period for Section 8 certificates, which provide not only rental assistance but also wide freedom of choice as to where a family lives, is almost three years. Even when families are lucky enough to obtain Section 8 certificates, however, not all landlords will honor them—a sign of the stigma that dogs the lives of poor people throughout the nation.

Estimates of the number of people who are homeless on any given night range between 600,000 and 760,000 nationwide. Funding to help the homeless has not kept pace with the growing need. Little wonder, then, that—despite an increase in shelter beds and food pantries—many requests for shelter and food go unmet. In addition, another advocacy group, the National Coalition for the Homeless, has pointed out that much of the existing funding focuses on emergency measures rather than on addressing the causes of homelessness. One hopeful sign is that, thanks to a substantial budget increase, the Department of Housing and Urban Development is now able to provide housing vouchers for 90,000 more families.

Although the causes of homelessness are complex, the principal ones remain jobs that do not pay a living wage, inadequate financial assistance for those who cannot work, insufficient medical care for the mentally ill and addicted, and the lack of affordable housing. Until these are addressed, homelessness will be neither out of sight nor out of mind. Indeed, in its prediction for the new year, the mayors' survey found that almost all the 30 cities surveyed expect the demand for emergency shelter and food to quicken. Hunger and homelessness in a prosperous United States is a disgrace. Voters need to tell their local, state and national leaders that careful planning and funding must be focused on caring for these people in need. Trying to make them invisible is no solution.

"Rural homelessness is as prevalent as urban homelessness."

Homelessness Is a Problem in Rural Communities

Yvonne M. Vissing

Contrary to popular stereotypes, just as many homeless reside in rural areas as on city streets, holds Yvonne M. Vissing in the following viewpoint. Because few homeless shelters exist in rural areas, she writes, the number of rural homeless people cannot easily be counted and is usually underestimated. Many of the rural homeless are children, who suffer extreme educational, health, and emotional problems as a result of homelessness. Vissing is the author of *Out of Sight, Out of Mind: Homeless Children and Families in Small-Town America*.

As you read, consider the following questions:
1. Who make up the rural homeless, as claimed by Vissing?
2. What emotional troubles may homeless children experience, in the author's view?
3. According to Vissing, why do the rural poor have trouble finding affordable housing?

Excerpted from "Homeless Children: Addressing the Challenge in Rural Schools," by Yvonne M. Vissing, *ERIC Digest*, November 1998. Reprinted by permission of the author.

The image of the homeless as predominantly single, adult males begging on city streets persists as a national stereotype. The stereotype implies almost nothing about K–12 schooling and prompts very little concern among rural people. Nonetheless, rural homelessness is as prevalent as urban homelessness. It differs markedly from the national stereotype. This viewpoint considers (1) the challenge of homelessness in rural areas, (2) the meaning of homelessness for rural children, (3) the educational problems of homelessness, and (4) causes of rural homelessness. . . .

The Challenge of Homelessness in Rural Areas

According to the National Coalition for the Homeless, "Studies comparing urban and rural homeless populations have shown that homeless people in rural areas are more likely to be white, female, married, currently working, homeless for the first time, and homeless for a shorter period of time." Vissing (1996) estimates that half of rural homeless households are families with children, both two-parent and single-parent families. She also suggests that female-headed households are about twice as numerous among rural, as compared to urban, homeless (32% vs. 16%).

Exact national figures are not available because 1990 census data on the homeless are doubtful, especially for rural areas. The census enumeration relied on the assumption that the homeless would be found in shelters. However, few shelters exist in rural areas. Even where shelters exist, rural homeless people favor other options because of shame and pride. Vissing (1996) reports that instead of relying on social agencies, rural homeless people move in temporarily with family or friends until they get back on their feet: 41% in rural areas versus 11% in urban areas.

Homelessness, then, arguably presents a more pressing challenge for rural than for urban educators because of the higher rate of homelessness involving families and children. But it receives far less attention, either from national media or from rural education and social authorities. Most available resources have been developed for the urban context.

Vissing (1996) uses the terms *housing displacement* and *housing distress* to describe rural homelessness. She defines rural homelessness as "lack of a consistent, safe physical structure and the *emotional deprivation that occurs as a result*" [italics added]. In rural areas, extended families are sometimes able to take in homeless young families. Abandoned houses can sometimes be occupied for free, but the availability of electricity, heating, and water supplies may be doubtful.

Housing shelters humans from the elements, but homes provide more. The social construct of "the home" describes the physical and emotional space needed for sustaining a private life. In educationally relevant terms, homelessness deprives children of the security they need to be themselves. Rural homelessness, which undermines the conditions of learning, is just one of many serious threats that poverty inflicts on children's ability to learn.

Educational Problems of Homeless Children and Youth

A diversity of people with possible rights to elementary and secondary educational services comprise the homeless: young children, single teenagers on their own (e.g., pregnant teens, teen parents, runaways), and young adults. Failure to provide *appropriate* educational services for these people magnifies their misfortune and frustrates the growth of their intellectual capacities.

Just enrolling homeless children in school and ensuring their attendance can be difficult. Residency requirements bar homeless children from attending school in 60% of the states. Other obstacles to admission include missing health and education records. Seventy percent of the states report difficulties getting records of homeless children who transfer to their schools. Often, homeless children need to be reimmunized. These obstacles are falling in many places, but the rural situation is unclear.

Although many homeless rural children continue to do well in school, transience, uncertainty, and emotional turmoil strongly undermine success. Many, perhaps most, homeless students will develop physical, behavioral, and emotional problems including post-traumatic stress disorders, depression, and anxiety.

Existing health problems may go untreated, and the stressors of homelessness inevitably produce new health problems. Transience may disrupt the task of preparing and serving regular meals. Quantity and quality of food commonly suffer as well.

According to the National Coalition for the Homeless (1997), rural as compared to urban homelessness involves more prevalent domestic violence but less substance abuse. These trends probably reflect the elevated rates of family homelessness in rural areas.

Understanding Rural Homelessness

Understanding rural homelessness requires a more flexible definition of homelessness. There are far fewer shelters in rural areas; therefore, people experiencing homelessness are less likely to live on the street or in a shelter, and more likely to live in a car or camper, or with relatives in overcrowded or substandard housing. Restricting definitions of homelessness to include only those who are literally homeless—that is, on the streets or in shelters—does not fit well with the rural reality, and also may exclude many rural communities from accessing federal dollars to address homelessness.

National Coalition for the Homeless, October 1997.

Profound emotional troubles accompany homelessness. Some children feel guilty, as if they were the cause of their families' poverty. They may also resent their parents for not being better providers. And they may actively resent other students, teachers, and administrators for not understanding homelessness. Self-destructive behaviors and psychic numbing are common. Homeless children may act out to get needed attention, but withdrawal is more common. Suicidal tendencies increase with homelessness, as do incidences of unplanned pregnancies and sexually transmitted diseases.

Children usually hide their homelessness. Among all others who interact with children, teachers are in the best position to identify problems unobtrusively. They observe their students carefully from day to day.

Causes of Rural Homelessness

Some observers note the persistent belief that the poor exhibit bad genes, poor planning, weakness, and overall lack of discipline and worthiness. According to this view, the moral fiber of the nation is decaying, and the character of the family is one victim; the poor reveal themselves as the worst citizens and the worst people, though it is important to distinguish between the deserving and the undeserving poor even in this explanation. Rural educators should understand that this concept may characterize conventional wisdom in many traditional communities.

This view has more national influence than educators might like. It helps the United States sustain a high level of *corporate* welfare, and, compared to other industrialized nations, a low level of *social* welfare.

Among many educators, an economic argument offers a more acceptable explanation. Homelessness is increasing, according to this argument, in part, because the income gap between rich and poor in the United States has widened substantially in recent decades. Measured in constant dollars, the *poorest* one-fifth of all families had incomes 9% lower in 1996 as compared to 1973. But incomes for the *wealthiest* one-fifth of all families rose 35%. The gap between rural and urban incomes is also widening, with the rural percentage of the average urban income falling from 78.5% in 1980 to 72.8% in 1990.

Child poverty is also increasing. The Children's Defense Fund (1998) reports that while the median income (in constant 1996 dollars) of U.S. families with children stayed level at $41,000 from 1976 to 1996, income for childless families rose 18% over the same period, and income for young families (parents under 30) sank 33%—from $30,000 to less than $20,000. The child poverty rate in young families doubled between 1973 and 1996, from 20% to 41%. And, in rural areas, child poverty rates are reportedly higher than in urban areas.

As the rural poor get poorer, the proportion of income claimed by housing goes up. By the standards of the 1950s, 20% of income constituted a normal housing expense. In the 1970s, the official standard was raised to 25%. Today, the standard is 30%. But the poor spend a larger proportion of their income on housing—often twice as large. Janet M. Fitchen (1981) suggests suburbanization has driven up the price of housing for the rural poor. As new residents move in, rural land and housing prices increase along with taxes. The supply of inexpensive housing shrinks, and new residents seek to increase housing standards. This process makes it difficult for the rural poor to live either in makeshift housing or mobile homes.

"Trends in the number of single-parent families in extreme poverty . . . suggest a large increase in the population of potentially homeless families since 1975."

Homelessness Is a Problem Among Women and Children

Eugene M. Lewit and Linda Schuurmann Baker

Although the number of homeless families and children is difficult to gauge, claim Eugene M. Lewit and Linda Schuurmann Baker in the following viewpoint, evidence suggests that homelessness and extreme poverty among families has risen dramatically since 1975. The increase in poor households led by single parents is the main cause of homelessness among women and children, contend the authors. Lewit is the director of research and grants for economics at the Center for the Future of Children, an organization that supports research and policy analysis in three areas: health, child development, and child abuse and neglect. Baker is a research analyst at the Center for the Future of Children.

As you read, consider the following questions:

1. Who makes up the typical homeless family with children, as stated by Lewit and Baker?
2. How many children are homeless, as estimated by the U.S. General Accounting Office and reported by the authors?
3. According to the authors, by how much did the number of poor households headed by single parents increase between 1974 and 1991?

Excerpted from "Homeless Families and Children," by Eugene M. Lewit and Linda Schuurmann Baker, *The Future of Children*, vol. 6, no. 2, Fall 1996. Adapted with the permission of the David and Lucile Packard Foundation.

Public concern about homelessness in the United States has increased in recent years. A late 1995 Gallup poll found that 86% of Americans feel sympathy for the homeless, and 33% report that they feel more sympathy now than they did five years ago. According to the same poll, one reason for this apparent increase in sympathy is that 17% of Americans, primarily women and young adults, believe that they could become homeless. The fact that these groups are concerned about homelessness reflects, in part, two decades of increases in the visibility of homeless women and children in the United States. Published reports suggest that most homeless families with children are headed by single women between the ages of 26 and 30 who have never been married and have two children.

Because shelter is a basic human need, it is not surprising that the effects of homelessness on children and families appear to be harsh and multifaceted. According to one study, homeless women are significantly more likely to have low birth weight babies than are similar poor women who are housed. Others report that, compared to the general population of children, homeless children have twice as many health problems, are more likely to go hungry, and have higher rates of developmental delay; and although findings have not been consistent, higher rates of depression, anxiety, and behavior problems have been reported for homeless children. . . .

Estimates of the size of the homeless population vary, depending on the definition of homelessness used. Even when definitions are clear and consistent, the methods used to count the homeless differ widely. Estimates of the number of homeless at one point in time or for a period of time can be made. In practice, homeless families and children are a difficult group to find and track, and few estimates that focus on children specifically have been made. Using a variety of techniques, the U.S. General Accounting Office (GAO) estimated that between 80,000 and 400,000 children were likely to be homeless or doubled up, living with friends and extended family, on any given night in 1988. Based on the GAO's "best" estimates, many more children were doubled up (186,000 in 1988) than living in shelters or other community settings provided for homeless families (68,000 in

1988). The length of homelessness for families tends to be short (less than three months), although there is evidence that a small group of families is homeless for years. Data on trends in actual homelessness are not available, but trends in the number of single-parent families in extreme poverty, conditions that tend to precede homelessness for families, suggest a large increase in the population of potentially homeless families since 1975. . . .

Trends in Homelessness for Children and Families

Although most agree that the numbers of homeless families and children have increased dramatically since the late 1970s, no data provide consistent estimates of the number of literally homeless families over time. Similarly, no data directly measure trends in the number of families with children that are doubled up or otherwise precariously housed. However, past studies have shown that homeless families with children tend to be headed by single parents who are very poor, and time series data are available on these families. These data can be used to infer trends in the number of precariously housed families with children and families at risk for literal homelessness. . . .

The number of households headed by single parents with personal incomes below 51% of the poverty line rose from more than 1 million in 1974 to about 2.5 million in 1991. In 1991, 50% of the poverty level for a household of three was $4,996, or $425 per month. At this income level, many of these families are probably at high risk of becoming literally homeless. It is not unreasonable, then, to expect that the number of homeless families with children increased between 1974 and 1991 in response to the 150% increase in this population of high-risk families during that time. Most of the increase in the population of single-parent families with incomes below 51% of the poverty line occurred between 1976 and 1983. In the early 1980s, attention began to focus on a "new" type of homeless population that included, for the first time since the Depression, visible numbers of women and children. Also noteworthy is the fact that the number of families in this at-risk category has not increased substantially since the early 1980s. (The increases in 1990 and 1991 probably were related to the recession in those years. Although data for more recent years are not shown, other reports indicate that the number of families with children with incomes below the poverty level has declined since 1991 coincident with the recent economic expansion.) Absent a clear trend in the population of families with children at risk for homelessness, it is difficult to know how much credence to give the anecdotal reports that this population has continued to increase in most recent years.

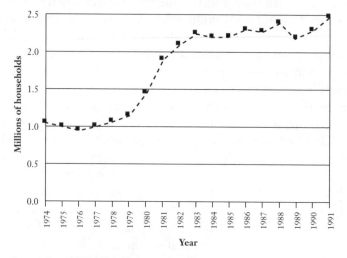

Number of Households with Children Headed by Single Parents with Personal Incomes Below 51% of the Poverty Line, 1974–1991

Source: Rossi, P.H. "Troubling Families: Family Homelessness in America," *American Behavioral Scientist* (January 1994) 37, 3:349, Figure 2.

Reliable information about the size, distribution, and composition of the homeless population is essential for effective planning for the housing, jobs, and public support homeless people need. Getting the necessary data, however, has proven to be extraordinarily difficult and controversial. As this review has emphasized, these obstacles stem in part from the nature of homelessness itself. The fact that a significant component of the homeless population of families with children includes those doubled up or precariously housed, a group not nearly as visible as the literally homeless but one whose housing arrangements are unstable, only complicates matters further.

Causes Are Not Well Understood

Although the statistical data on homelessness are spotty, it is well accepted that homelessness has increased for U.S. families over the past two decades, with most of the growth concentrated in the 1980s. In the 1950s and 1960s, researchers studying urban homelessness did not find or mention homeless families. Today, however, no matter which estimates are used, researchers conclude that counts of both homeless individuals and homeless families have increased dramatically since that time. The causes of this growth in the number of homeless families are multiple, complex, and not well understood. Rising rates of family homelessness are probably related to the increase in the number of families in extreme poverty in the 1970s and 1980s combined with a substantial expansion in the number of single-parent families. The increase in poverty, however, cannot be the whole story because poverty rates among families with children were much higher in the 1950s and early 1960s than in recent years, but homelessness for families with children was not widely visible during the earlier period.

Given the large number of families at economic and social risk for homelessness, it has been hypothesized that estimates of the number of homeless families, and perhaps family homelessness itself, are at least partially determined by the shelter system. The population of identified literally homeless families consists almost entirely of families in shelters, and most estimates of the homeless population build on statistics from shelter operations. Accordingly, shelter capacity plays a crucial role in determining the size of the population of homeless families. By providing a refuge, shelters may actually lower the threshold for what families are willing to tolerate in their daily lives before becoming homeless. For example, in the absence of shelter alternatives, women abused by their partners may not perceive any viable alternative to remaining. With an increased availability of battered-women's and other family shelters, some such women may be able to remove themselves and their children from abusive home-based relationships. A byproduct of this important process would be an increase in the shelter (hence homeless) population.

Solving the problem of family homelessness will require multiple strategies and changes in broad economic trends—no easy task. The lack of good data on the population of homeless children and their families, however, cannot be used as an excuse for not addressing the problem. Whether there are 41,000 literally homeless children on any given night, as is suggested by the GAO report, or more than 10 times that number, as asserted by some advocacy groups, homelessness among children indicates that society is not functioning at a level that assures at least minimally decent basic necessities for all children. The new data on annual unduplicated counts of the homeless suggest that many more poor families may cycle through homelessness each year than point-in-time estimates indicate. This fact should increase concern for this population, as should the finding that, although homelessness is not a permanent condition for most homeless families, many children experience this state for a substantial portion of their young lives.

Most initial governmental responses to the emergence of literal homelessness did not address the root causes of homelessness, but instead provided emergency aid intended to help people survive during their homeless experience. However, the data on the number of families at risk for literal homelessness suggest that the pool of these families is so large that solutions that focus only on trying to help families after they become literally homeless will not substantially reduce the overall number of homeless families and may, to a certain extent, increase that population. In this environment, although these programs of emergency assistance are very much needed, policies focused on the much larger problem of reducing the number of families at risk for homelessness, very poor families with limited social supports, will be necessary to reduce or eliminate homelessness among families with children.

"Homelessness is almost exclusively a male problem."

Homelessness Is a Serious Problem Among Men

Anthony Browne

In the subsequent viewpoint, Anthony Browne, a writer for the British publication *New Statesman*, asserts that homelessness is primarily a male problem. Men make up the vast majority of groups that commonly experience homelessness, including the unemployed, former prisoners, veterans of the armed forces, and members of the foster care system. Furthermore, states Browne, men's friendships tend to be less intimate than women's, which makes men less likely to seek help from friends during times of financial trouble.

As you read, consider the following questions:
1. Why are women less likely than men to be officially homeless, in Browne's view?
2. According to the author, why are foster care boys more likely than girls to leave care and end up on the streets?
3. How do men typically cope with their problems, in the author's opinion?

John is not typical of the homeless. Well educated and articulate, he has slept rough for five years, ever since his wife died. Since his loss, John has sought refuge in the bottle; he has lost his job as a teacher and his home. He looks 70, with what can only be described as weathered features—but he is in fact 51. He clings to dignity by describing himself as a "park-bench poet"—with some justification: he hassles public librarians to get copies of Heinrich Heine in the original German (apparently the translations don't convey the angst of the original). He gives a share of the money he gets from begging to some pensioners he knows. They need it more than him, he says, because he has no bills to pay.

In reality, John is actually typical in his atypicality. Homeless people are almost as diverse a group as the population at large. There is only one thing that almost all of them have in common, apart from the lack of a home: they are male.

A Male Problem

As any walk through any city centre at night will show you, homelessness is almost exclusively a male problem. According to the Homeless Network, an umbrella organisation for homeless charities, around 89 per cent of those sleeping rough are men.

Ask any housing expert to explain the discrepancy and, surprisingly, they will tell you that no research has been done on the subject. The housing charity Crisis has recently started addressing the gender aspect of homelessness; it's just commissioned a report into "Homelessness and Women".

One clear reason is that the street is a more dangerous place for women than men. All those sleeping rough are liable to be beaten up by drunk people leaving pubs, but women are especially vulnerable and tend to make more use of emergency accommodation. But even in these "direct-access shelters", men still outnumber women four to one.

Four to one. Compare that to eight to one on the street. Like public toilets, direct-shelter beds are almost all allocated by gender, and there are roughly twice as many emergency beds available for women sleeping rough as there are for men. The end result is inevitable: while there are often vacancies for women's accommodation, for men the shelters are usually full.

"There are nights when there are no male spaces available, so the men go rough, while there are still spaces available for women," says Kate Tomlinson, manager of policy at Crisis. Put another way, it's common for homeless men to turn up at emergency accommodation and be told, in effect, "If you were a woman, we'd have a bed for you."

Women—particularly young ones—are also less likely to be officially homeless because they are liable to be drawn into prostitution or abusive relationships that have the one saving grace of taking them off the street.

The main economic cause of homelessness is unemployment. The destruction of male-dominated unskilled manual jobs and the creation of female-dominated service jobs have left many men at a disadvantage in the labour market. Government figures show that men are twice as likely to be unemployed as women, and three times as likely to be long-term unemployed. Homelessness is often only a step away.

Routes into Homelessness Are Dominated by Men

"The routes into homelessness are dominated by men," says Tomlinson. "Whether it's prisoners being released to the outside world, soldiers leaving the armed forces, young people leaving care, dependency on alcohol or drugs, or losing accommodation after the breakdown of a relationship, men outnumber women."

There are 20 times as many male prisoners as female ones; and according to the National Association for the Care and Resettlement of Offenders, half of them have no home to go to after release. The probation service does its best to arrange accommodation, but admits it often just can't cope.

"The probation service is not an accommodation agency, and we can't guarantee that people find a place to stay. We'll try, but there are times you can't even get emergency accommodation," said a spokesman for the Inner London Probation Service, the largest in the country. He added: "It can happen that people spend their last night of their sentence in prison, and then spend the next night on the street." This is not nice for the former prisoner—and especially not nice for society: it is difficult to think of any way more likely to make a former prisoner re-offend than chucking them out on the street.

The prison story is repeated with another great institution of the state: the army. Roughly one in five of those sleeping rough ended up on the streets after leaving the armed forces with nowhere to stay. Again, it's almost all men. "You just don't find homeless women soldiers," says Tomlinson.

Shopping Cart Soldiers

After my return from Vietnam, I wandered around the world for almost 12 years, confused, not knowing what was wrong. I felt dead inside, empty, numbed. I remember wet, lonely nights feeling nothing but absolute desolation. I remember sitting on park benches at night watching the passersby, envious that they had such fine lives. I was cold and lonely, wishing I could see my family, wishing that I had a family to go home to. From time to time, I would find an odd job as a construction worker which, of course, would afford me the opportunity to rent a room in a residential hotel for a few days, or perhaps even a few weeks.

But for the most part, it was the streets among the other homeless veterans, my friends, the other shopping cart soldiers. We were a growing army with no mission, no encampment.

John Mulligan, *American Legion Magazine*, October 1998.

Soldiers need far more help than is usually realised, according to David Warner, director of the Homeless Network. "If you've been a squaddie for ten years and everything has been done for you and your life has been organised for you, then what you need is rehabilitation." The army isn't totally oblivious, according to Tomlinson: "It gives them a book," she says ironically.

The picture is similar, if less extreme, in care: young men in foster homes or institutions outnumber young women by roughly three to two; of those who leave care and end up on the streets, boys outnumber girls by about four to one. Peter Hardman, the director of First Key, sees many reasons for this. Boys, for one, are more likely to fight and then fall out with their foster families than girls. "Young women leaving care are more readily accepted back into the immediate or extended foster family," says Hardman. "There are more young women who have converted the foster place-ment into lodging."

Pregnancy, too, plays its part. Various studies show that between one-seventh and one-quarter of young women who leave care are already mothers, and local authorities are legally required to give them accommodation. Hardman says: "All sorts of child-protection issues come to the fore—they're in the safety net. Many local authorities have mother and baby units. Young men who are fathers don't tend to stay with the children and don't get accommodation."

Many of those involved with the homeless mention this legal assistance in explaining the difference in homelessness rates between men and women. Nicholas Pleace of the Centre for Housing Policy at the University of York says: "Homeless women are far more likely to be with children, and thus tend to get assisted under legislation. The only other way of getting statutory assistance is by being classified as 'vulnerable', such as having mental health problems—but that's so much more difficult to identify."

Men's Inability to Help Themselves

Yet institutional and legal issues alone don't explain the ex-treme disparity between the number of homeless men and women; what does emerge from this grim picture of gen-der inequality is men's inability to help themselves in times of crisis.

Megan Ravenhill, a researcher at the Centre for the Study of Social Exclusion at the London School of Economics, has recently been interviewing homeless people about their lives, and says a clear pattern is emerging: women have bet-ter, stronger social support networks. "Women tend to spend longer sleeping on friends' floors because they're less likely to fall out with their friends. They're more likely to have a network of friends from antenatal classes, the nursery or the school gate. For men, friendships tend to be based around work, so that once they've lost their job, they lose their social network."

Men's friendships tend to be less intimate and thus less supportive in times of crisis, says Ravenhill, whereas women are more likely to be able to help each other in practical ways because they know friends who have been through it all before and learnt the lessons. "Lots of the men just don't know what to do, how to find hostels or help. They feel totally alone," she says.

Instead of relying on friends, men have other—far more destructive—ways of coping. If marriages fail or they lose their jobs, pride often stops them asking for help, and they are far more likely to turn to drink or drugs. Homelessness beckons; the risk of suicide rises.

Children can also be a stabilising factor in women's lives. Many people become homeless after their marriage or relationship breaks down; when children are involved, it is far more likely that it is the man who leaves and has to find somewhere else.

But social attitudes take little of this into account. Men are meant to be strong and should be able to look after themselves—otherwise it's all their fault. "There's a lot of stereotyping that goes on—it's almost the Victorian idea of the undeserving poor, particularly with male rough sleepers," says Pleace, "and because of the way we think about homelessness, they're seen as an undeserving group."

Periodical Bibliography

The following articles have been selected to supplement the diverse views presented in this chapter. Addresses are provided for periodicals not indexed in the *Readers' Guide to Periodical Literature*, the *Alternative Press Index*, the *Social Sciences Index*, or the *Index to Legal Periodicals and Books*.

America	"Homeless Children," November 13, 1999.
Patricia Bailey	"Oh, Canada," *Toward Freedom*, March–August 1999.
Skip Barry	"Homeless at Fifty-Five," *Commonweal*, April 23, 1999.
Nina Bernstein	"With a Job, Without a Home," *The New York Times*, March 4, 1999.
Warren Caragata	"Homelessness Is Fixable," *Maclean's*, January 25, 1999.
Patricia Chrisholm	"'This Is a Human Problem,'" *Maclean's*, March 23, 1998.
Lynne Duke	"Homeless and Hiding," *Washington Post National Weekly Edition*, December 20–27, 1999. Available from Reprints, 1150 15th St. NW, Washington, DC 20071.
Ralph S. Hambrick and Gary T. Johnson	"The Future of Homelessness," *Society*, September/October 1998.
Bob Herbert	"Children in Crisis," *The New York Times*, June 10, 1999.
Kari Lyderson	"Out of Sight," *In These Times*, June 12, 2000.
Ralph Nunez and Cybelle Fox	"A Snapshot of Family Homelessness Across America," *Political Science Quarterly*, Summer 1999.
William Raspberry	"Is the Homeless Crisis Over or Are We Indifferent?" *Liberal Opinion Week*, October 19, 1998. Available from PO Box 880, Vinton, IA 52348-0880.
Romesh Ratnesar	"Not Gone, but Forgotten?" *Time*, February 8, 1999.
Catherine Walsh	"Street Children Around the World," *America*, September 17, 1997.

CHAPTER 2

What Are the Causes of Homelessness?

Chapter Preface

In 1996, with bipartisan support, President Bill Clinton signed welfare reform into law, ending Aid to Families with Dependent Children (AFDC), a federal program established under Franklin D. Roosevelt that provided cash benefits to needy single mothers. The reformed program, Temporary Assistance to Needy Families (TANF), distributes money to states based on their success at moving welfare recipients into jobs. TANF requires welfare recipients to find work within two years; limits cash benefits to five years; and places more stringent restrictions on who can receive Social Security Income benefits and food stamps.

Although TANF has only recently taken effect, some researchers report that the program is already causing a dramatic increase in homelessness. According to Julie Dworkin, a policy specialist for the Chicago Coalition for the Homeless, 25 percent of welfare recipients in Michigan became homeless after losing their benefits; in Ohio, homelessness jumped 17 percent within six months of benefit reductions. Even worse, claim opponents of welfare reform, many former AFDC recipients who have found jobs are homeless nonetheless because they do not earn enough to meet housing costs.

Supporters of the new reforms, on the other hand, argue that the negative effects of TANF—including the rise in homelessness—have been overstated. Douglas J. Becharov and Peter Germanis, directors of the Welfare Reform Academy, state that "happily, there is no evidence that welfare reform has caused substantial increases in homelessness or other indicators of extreme hardship. . . . [D]espite extensive efforts, journalists have found few individual horror stories of the harmful effects of welfare reform." Instead, maintain proponents, TANF has been overwhelmingly successful: As of late 1999, welfare rolls were down forty percent and most former recipients were working, earning an average of $5.50 to $7.50 per hour.

The debate over welfare reform's impact on homelessness and other issues related to the causes of homelessness will be discussed in the following chapter.

"Working homeless people report that their incomes are not sufficient to afford a family's basic living needs."

Low Wages and Limited Employment Opportunities Cause Homelessness

Aimee Molloy

Aimee Molloy is a writer for the Center for Poverty Solutions, a nonprofit charitable organization dedicated to eliminating the root causes of poverty. In the viewpoint that follows, she contends that low wages and limited employment opportunities force poor people into homelessness. Close to one-fifth of the homeless population works, Molloy holds, but still cannot afford to pay for housing. Furthermore, homeless people face severe barriers to employment, including limited opportunities for low-skilled workers, the high costs of transportation and child care, and poor health.

As you read, consider the following questions:
1. Who are the homeless, according to the author?
2. What examples does Molloy provide to support her argument that the minimum wage is too low to meet housing costs?
3. How have changes in the high-tech industry affected work opportunities, as explained by the author?

Excerpted from "Helping People Off the Streets: Real Solutions to Urban Homelessness," by Aimee Molloy, from the website of the Center for Poverty Solutions, www.ctrforpovertysolutions.org/public/campus.htm. Reprinted with permission.

The word "homeless" has become the generally accepted term for people sleeping in our city parks and panhandling in our downtown areas. It is also used to define a mother of three who was forced out of her home because of domestic violence; a person with schizophrenia who was released from a stable, supervised environment fifteen years ago; a veteran, disabled in Vietnam, who returned home unable to work and struggling with an addiction; and a family of five in which both parents work but cannot afford to pay rent, cover medical expenses and provide food for their family on minimum wage earnings. . . .

Why Don't People Just Get a Job?

In our current time of economic prosperity in the United States, many people are enjoying greater wealth, higher earnings and profitable investments. Unemployment rates are reported to be low, wages high. So why don't people who are homeless just get a job? Logic tells us that if these people worked, they would have more money and could afford housing. Since they are homeless, it is easy to assume they would rather not work, but choose to remain that way.

First, it is important to understand that nearly one out of five homeless Americans do work, either full- or part-time. A 1998 survey of Baltimore's homeless found that 17% of those surveyed were employed and approximately 46% had lost their jobs within the [previous] year. So what keeps the working poor from being able to afford rent? And what factors account for people becoming or remaining unemployed when our economy is thriving?

Minimum Wage. Inadequate wages put housing out of reach for many workers. Working homeless people report that their incomes are not sufficient to afford a family's basic living needs. Under the current [1998] minimum wage, the income earned by a full-time worker equals 85% of the estimated poverty line for a family of three.

As recently as 1967, a person working full-time at minimum wage earned enough to raise a family of three above the poverty line. However, between 1981 and 1990, the minimum wage remained at $3.35 per hour. During this same period, the cost of living rose 48%. In 1996, Congress raised the minimum wage to $5.15 per hour, but the increase only slightly made up for the loss due to inflation in the 1980s.

In every state, more than the minimum wage is needed to allow a family to afford a one- or two-bedroom apartment at Fair Market Rent. According to the National Coalition for the Homeless, in the median state a minimum wage worker would have to work 83 hours per week to afford a two-bedroom apartment at 30% of their income, the federal definition of affordable housing.

Homeless Parents' Reasons for Current Unemployment*†

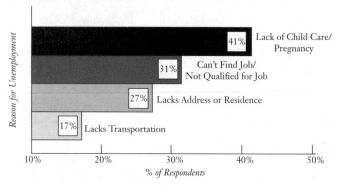

Respondents could give multiple answers; all percentages do not add to 100.

†*Of the remaining categories, illness/disability/substance abuse was cited by 15% and welfare pays more, doesn't want to work, and language problem were each cited by 3%. Another 14% cited other unspecified reasons for unemployment.*

Ralph Nunez and Cybelle Fox, *Political Science Quarterly*, Summer 1999.

Recent policy discussions have focused on creating a "living wage" which is defined as the minimum income needed for an individual or family to be able to meet their basic needs: housing, food, health care, transportation and clothing. Economists have determined the living wage in Maryland to be $7.70 per hour.

A Wider Wage Gap. The concept of earning such an inadequate income may be unfamiliar to many people at the higher end of the earnings spectrum, as the wages of highly-skilled workers are steadily increasing. According to a recent report by the U.S. Department of Labor, from 1983 to 1996 the inflation-adjusted hourly wages of workers in the top one-tenth of the workforce increased from $24.80 to $25.75 per hour. Concurrently, wages for workers in the bottom one-tenth of the workforce fell from $6.28 per hour to $5.46. Adjusting for benefits, highly paid workers gained $1.73 per hour during this period in inflation-adjusted total compensation, while low-end workers lost 93 cents per hour. Additionally, 90% of low-wage workers did not receive any paid leave.

Limited Employment Opportunities. The recent progress made in the high-tech industry has created many new jobs paying high salaries, and the resulting benefits to businesses and skilled workers are numerous. However, there has been a decline in work opportunities for low-skilled workers, mainly due to a loss of well-paying manufacturing jobs. The majority of employment options for poorly-educated or low-skilled people are in the service industry. These jobs pay less and are less secure. Because of this, we have seen an unprecedented incidence of chronic unemployment and underemployment.

Barriers to Existing Jobs

Transportation. In Baltimore, transportation was listed as the major barrier to employment during a survey of homeless families and individuals. According to the U.S. Department of Housing and Urban Development's report on the state of American Cities in 1998, our suburbs are experiencing a rapid job growth. However, this has created a "spatial mismatch" as many poor people do not have the resources to get to the higher paying entry-level jobs in the suburbs. Few poor families own cars, and public transportation systems in many large cities such as Baltimore do not provide adequate service into the lower density suburban job centers. Also, the increasing cost of public transportation is a significant expenditure for a family earning a very limited income.

Child Care. Safe and affordable child care is necessary to allow parents to work. However, affordable child care remains out of reach for many working poor or unemployed families. While the federal government has created programs to help poor families with child care expenses as part of recent welfare reform initiatives, only 10% of the families who qualify for federal child care receive assistance. Many cities have tens of thousands of people on waiting lists for child care programs. While the average American family pays about 7% of its income on child care expenses, 25% of low-income families' incomes go toward child care costs.

Health Care. Poor health keeps people from being able to secure or maintain employment. Anyone who has worked with a toothache, had a headache or had to depend on crutches for a broken limb can understand the importance of good health in doing a good job at work. Of the homeless people surveyed in Baltimore city shelters in 1998, 46% reported living with a disability and 38% rated their health as fair or poor. To make matters worse, more than a third of people living in poverty have no health insurance of any kind and therefore are unable to receive the primary or preventive care they need.

"The 'will nots'. . . are voluntary street people. Homeless by choice, opportunists, they know a good thing when they see it."

Homelessness Is Often Voluntary

Bob Klug

In the following viewpoint, Bob Klug argues that although some people are homeless due to circumstances beyond their control, others simply choose to be homeless. This latter group, which Klug calls the "will nots," are drunks who enjoy living on the streets. The generosity of average Americans, he maintains, allows the "will nots" to maintain their lazy, irresponsible lifestyle. Klug is the associate director for the North County Interfaith Council, a group of faith communities that have joined together to address poverty and homelessness in north San Diego County.

As you read, consider the following questions:

1. What three distinct groups make up the homeless population, in Klug's view?
2. Describe the lifestyle of voluntary street people, as portrayed by the author.
3. According to the author, what can society do to prevent homelessness?

Reprinted, with permission, from "Help the Needy—Boot the Greedy," by Bob Klug, *North County Times*, December 6, 1998.

Three separate and very distinct groups of people make up the homeless population—the "cannots," the "have nots" and the "will nots."

The "cannots" are the mentally ill. Severely handicapped, they deserve the help to which any disabled citizen is entitled. These poor souls are at the bottom of society's barrel and their plight is a national disgrace.

The "have nots" are parents with children. Usually a young single mother with two children, they desperately need and deserve our help. It is a grim time for their family and they will never forget this holiday season.

The "Will Nots"

The "will nots," though, are voluntary street people. Homeless by choice, opportunists, they know a good thing when they see it. They have it made—and they have got to go.

Street people hang together and everyone knows everyone. They have their own rules, protocols and street justice. It's a vibrant life, sprinkled with flashes of the dreaded delirium tremens and outrageous street happenings. These folks relish scams, abandoned buildings, easy rip-offs and take delight in sharing their stories of derring-do.

Most wake up at the crack of dawn and rummage through trash bins for aluminum cans, glass bottles and plastic containers. The pickin's are good, by golly, and those little gems are money.

About 11 A.M. it's time to cash in at a local recycling center, then make a beeline to the nearest liquor store where for $1.11 a 40-ounce bottle of malt liquor can be had. Then it's just a quick stop at a fast-food dumpster, chug a beer, and stagger off to meet with their cohorts.

The rest of the day is spent in an alcoholic stupor among friends, laughing, crying, joking and fumbling for change. As night falls they grab their bedrolls, take one last swig and pass out, content that their big, green treasure chests will be brimming with more goodies in the morning.

So what happens if they have a bad day "canning"? No problem: panhandle. Women are an easy mark and grocery store parking lots are a perfect venue. A bad day panhandling? No problem: One of the most lucrative scams is standing on a busy street corner with a sign that says "Will work for food."

How can the average American, unaware of the ruse, not feel a twinge of compassion? We feel sad and sorry for what seems to be a grim reflection of what we have become. We pride ourselves on helping those in need; we always have as individuals and as a nation. So we pull over and give the guy $5.

Have you ever seen a sign guy at 7 A.M. when work is available? Nope, the only time you'll see these crafty fellows is in the afternoon.

OK, let's pretend the trash bins are empty, there's a security guard in the grocery store parking lot, and it's too early to do the sign thing. What then? No problem: Street people care for each other and share with each other because each knows the special horror of going without.

Reprinted by permission of Chuck Asay and Creators Syndicate.

Of course, there are times when all else fails and that's when the regulars play their hole card: credit. Seedy-side liquor vendors take kindly to their best patrons. There isn't much profit in the girlie magazines, and cigarette sales are slumping, so Mr. Boozer is good for 40 ounces.

Rainy day? Not a problem, the dollar theater is open—two thumbs up! Nothing like spending a wet day at the movies, coughing that dumpster cough.

Oh, did I mention the Community Clinic is offering free TB tests to the public?

Now blend in the no-fault homeless and you have a turkey shoot for these predators. If a poor, old, mentally ill woman gets a Social Security check, you had better bet she will be queen for a day.

A frightened young woman with children?

In Escondido the highest concentration of the hard core is in the vicinity of Mission Avenue and Rock Springs Road. It's perfect. Apartment and motel dumpsters galore, recycling centers, two "cheap" liquor stores, nice grocery store, fast-food dumpsters, a floppy motel and some great hiding places. It just doesn't get any better for those who don't care about themselves or society.

What Society Can Do

So what can we do?

Ignore sign-holders and report panhandlers to business owners. Require fast-food restaurants to keep their dumpsters locked. Stake out the few liquor stores that are breaking the law by selling booze to known street drunks. Apartment managers must report dumpster divers to the police immediately, because in the canning racket, those big, green piggybanks hold the key to Pandora's box.

If we focus our efforts on these few choke points, the undeserving will leave on their own and wander off to the next community where the pickings are easy.

We can do this, and we must. There are too many among us freezing on the streets at night and in dire straits during the day. They need and deserve our immediate help.

| *"Skyrocketing rents are pushing working people to the brink of homelessness."*

Lack of Affordable Housing Causes Homelessness

Bruce Burleson

Bruce Burleson argues in the subsequent viewpoint that homelessness in the United States stems from the lack of affordable housing for the poor. In recent years, claims the author, inexpensive housing options such as single-room occupancy units and cubicle hotels have become scarce as rents and housing costs have skyrocketed. Consequently, many of the working poor cannot afford to provide homes for themselves and their families. Burleson is the Boston correspondent for the *People's Weekly World*, a newspaper that advocates socialism as a solution to society's problems.

As you read, consider the following questions:
1. According to Burleson, what is one common myth about the homeless?
2. What is the "catch-22" in the life of the homeless person, as explained by the author?
3. What evidence does the author provide to support his claim that current housing assistance programs are inadequate?

Excerpted from "Homelessness: Is There a Solution?" by Bruce Burleson, *People's Weekly World*, December 19, 1998. Reprinted with permission.

Homelessness is the condition of being without a permanent place to live—to sleep, eat, shower, come and go as one pleases, leave one's belongings, and receive one's mail. It is the condition of being without a place to call one's own home.

There are some 750,000 people without a place to stay on any given night in this country. Some two million people were homeless at some point in the past year. Boston alone has over 5,000 people living on the streets or in shelters; in New York City the number runs into the tens of thousands.

A pedestrian today can hardly walk very far in one of America's cities before encountering a homeless person—someone asking for spare change, selling a street newspaper, gathering cans and bottles for recycling, or sleeping under a blanket in the park.

The same pedestrian, will no doubt also see scores of abandoned buildings, boarded up and wasted, and then might wonder: Why is there homelessness in our society? And for that matter, why do some people live on giant estates complete with tennis courts and swimming pools, while others huddle in doorways or sleep in shelters? What has gone wrong in this country, supposedly the land of plenty?

Before these questions can be properly answered, it is important to cut through the thick web of misinformation and stereotypes that have been attached to homelessness over the years. The media, and the politicians who regularly utilize it to ramrod their reactionary agenda, have painted a negative portrait of the homeless.

The Stereotype of Homelessness

When the issue of homelessness is discussed, the image often portrayed of a homeless person is of a disheveled, dirty, lazy man sitting against a wall with a bottle of booze in his lap. This image of homelessness is a stereotype that is often used to blame the homelessness problem on its victims—the homeless people themselves.

The reality is that homeless people are like anyone you'll meet on the street: Black, white and Brown, male and female, young and old, employed and unemployed.

Consider a few statistics on the homeless:

- Some 20 to 40 percent of homeless people are employed.
- 37 percent are families with children. This is the fastest-growing population among the homeless.
- 25 percent are under the age of 18.
- 30 percent are over the age of 45.
- 25–30 percent are mentally disabled.
- 30–40 percent are drug or alcohol dependent.

These statistics clearly disprove the long-standing, mass media–fueled myth that homeless people are typically drunks, druggies or crazy. Even though 30–40 percent of the homeless are alcoholics or drug addicts, only 30–40 percent are, and although 25–30 percent are mentally disturbed, only 25–30 percent are. Moreover, millions of Americans who are alcoholics or mentally ill persons never become homeless. So, granted that while addiction or mental illness makes the threat of homelessness more serious, these problems only *contribute*—they do not *cause* homelessness.

One Common Myth About the Homeless

One common myth is that "most" homeless came out of the "deinstitutionalization" of mental hospitals. However, deinstitutionalization ended during the 1970s, and most people who are homeless today became so long after that.

The reality is that the causes of homelessness really have nothing to do with alcoholism, drug addiction, mental illness, "deinstitutionalization" or any of the issues that are typically associated with homelessness. Those things are not *causes* but are merely *contributing factors*. The causes of homelessness are two societal problems that are endemic in a capitalist, profit-driven society: lack of affordable housing, and extreme poverty.

There is a catch-22 in the life of the homeless person: it is nearly impossible to get a job without first having a permanent address and phone number, and getting a permanent address requires steady income—usually from a job! Shortages of both money on the part of the renter, and affordable dwellings to rent, perpetuate their problems.

Affordable housing in our country is dwindling. Between 1973 and 1993, 2.2 million low-rent apartment units have vanished from the market, while the demand for such units increased by 4.7 million renters. Between 1993 and 1995, the supply of low cost units decreased by another 900,000.

In addition to the loss of inexpensive apartment units, there has been a sharp decline in single-room occupancy (SRO) housing. Traditionally, SRO's have been used by homeless people—particularly those with mental health or addiction issues—to get off the streets, however temporarily. But between 1970 and the mid-1980's *one million* SRO's were demolished. This trend has been most notable in large cities: Chicago lost all of its cubicle hotels (rooms which could be rented for $8–$10 per night); New York City lost 87 percent of its $200 per month SRO stock; Los Angeles lost more than half of its SRO housing.

Reprinted by permission of Kirk Anderson.

Housing assistance programs, while a step in the right direction, have been inadequate. Only 26 percent of households eligible for housing assistance ever receive it. In 1997, the U.S. Conference of Mayors conducted a study of the status of hunger and homelessness. They found that public housing applicants wait an average of 19 months to receive assistance, and applicants for Section 8 housing vouchers wait an average of 37 months. In 19 of the cities surveyed, the waiting list for housing programs was so long that the cities actually stopped accepting applications!

Skyrocketing Rents

Skyrocketing rents are pushing working people to the brink of homelessness. In 1995, the city of Boston ended its rent-control law. Apartment units that once cost $500 per month now cost $900. A three-bedroom apartment in working-class South Boston currently rents for about $1,800 per month.

The conservative Boston landlords who advocated for the end of rent control claimed that it would be "good for everyone." They argued that ending rent control would lead to higher property-tax revenues and create incentives for developers to build new, more profitable housing units, eventually causing rent prices to fall again.

However, it is clear that, as the years go by after the end of rent control, housing costs have not fallen but have even doubled. Real-estate developers are building mainly expensive units and are also buying up older, affordable houses and refurbishing them into yuppie condominiums. So clearly, relying on the invisible hand of the housing market does not benefit poor people who need housing.

The result of the terrible shortage of affordable housing has been a sharp increase in homelessness and poverty. Despite the Department of Housing and Urban Development's "Fair Market Rent" standard—that a family should not pay more than 30 percent of its income on housing—most poor families have no choice. An average minimum-wage worker would have to work 83 hours a week in order to afford a two-bedroom apartment at 30 percent of her or his income.

The federal government has in the past taken notable stabs at the problem of homelessness. In 1987, the McKinney Act was passed, creating all kinds of new programs to house, feed, educate and help homeless people find jobs.

However, over the years pieces of the McKinney Act have remained underfunded or seriously underfunded.

> "*[Welfare] benefit cutoffs and reductions are beginning to kick in at different times all across the country. When they do, the result seems to be the same: more homeless families.*"

Welfare Cuts Have Increased Homelessness

Leslie Miller

In the following viewpoint, Associated Press writer Leslie Miller discusses the effects of recent legislative reforms that reduce—and in some cases eliminate—welfare benefits to single mothers with children. Since these policies have been implemented, she writes, homeless shelters have been flooded with former welfare recipients. Miller states that, according to research studies, cuts in public assistance are responsible for the sharp increase in homelessness in recent years.

As you read, consider the following questions:

1. As cited by Miller, what two reasons for the increase in homelessness did the U.S. Conference of Mayors offer?
2. What percentage of welfare recipients became homeless after losing some or all of their benefits, according to the study conducted by Homes for the Homeless?

Reprinted by permission of *Today's Homeowner Magazine* and The Associated Press from "Welfare Cuts Adding More Kids to Rolls of Homeless," by Leslie Miller, as found at the following URL: www.join-hands.com/welfare/homeless.html.

Volunteers have been wrapping thousands of sweaters, stuffed animals and Barbie dolls to give to 1,600 children during a holiday bash at the [Boston] Bayside Expo Center.

The kids will sing carols, eat goodies and ride ponies. The cheer will be short-lived, however, because after the party, more than half of the children will go back to homeless shelters.

The Effects of Welfare Reform

Every year, children are homeless, but advocates for the poor say the situation looks especially grim now, with the effects of the national overhaul of welfare just beginning to be felt.

The U.S. Conference of Mayors reported in 1999 that 15 percent more homeless families requested shelter this year than last. The mayors cited cuts in public assistance and the lack of affordable housing as two reasons for the increase.

In Massachusetts, many welfare recipients stand to lose their cash benefits as they come up against the two-year time limit imposed by the state's strict welfare reform law.

"The wolf may be approaching the door, but it's not there yet," said Philip Mangano, executive director of the Massachusetts Housing and Shelter Alliance. "It'll be bad enough soon enough."

More Homeless Families

Benefit cutoffs and reductions are beginning to kick in at different times all across the country. When they do, the result seems to be the same: more homeless families.

Almost half of welfare recipients in 10 cities became homeless between September 1997 and September 1998 after their benefits were reduced or eliminated, according to a survey conducted by Homes for the Homeless, a research center affiliated with Columbia University in New York City.

In Newark, N.J., shelters flooded with the working poor are closing because they are financed in large part by programs that don't subsidize people who work.

"If that's happening now in this great economy, what's going to happen when welfare reform kicks in?" said Cybelle Fox, a research associate for Homes for the Homeless.

A November 1998 study by the National Coalition for the Homeless found half of homeless families in Atlanta had recently lost welfare benefits. In Los Angeles, 12 percent of homeless families surveyed said they lost their place to live because of benefit cuts.

In one Wisconsin county, homelessness increased by 50 percent for children, but only 1 percent for adult men, a group largely unaffected by welfare reform.

"Almost all of our transitional facilities for women and children are full, have waiting lists and are turning people away," said Robert Hess, president of the Center for Poverty Solutions in Baltimore. "All our emergency shelters for women and children are full and turning people away."

AMERICA'S NEW SAFETY NET

Reprinted with permission from Rex Babin.

Hess is keeping a worried eye on January 1, 2000, when Maryland imposes its two-year welfare cutoff.

In Michigan, mothers who have had their benefits reduced or eliminated can't find jobs that pay enough for rent, health insurance, food and transportation, said Richard Anderson, program director for the Traveler's Aid Society of Detroit.

He thinks the Homes for the Homeless study actually underreports the number of families who lost their homes because of welfare reform.

Recently, Anderson's group hosted a party similar to the bash scheduled in Boston. About 1,500 homeless children showed up.

"The party was a success inasmuch as the kids had a place to go," Anderson said. "Now what are we going to do with these kids the other 364 days?"

"Approximately one-third of the single adult homeless population [has] a serious mental illness."

Mental Illness Contributes to Homelessness

Henry G. Cisneros

A large proportion of the homeless population suffers from a debilitating mental illness, maintains Henry G. Cisneros in the viewpoint that follows. Because the severely mentally ill cannot sustain a stable lifestyle without consistent treatment, he contends, many become homeless. The problem of the homeless mentally ill has worsened since the 1960s, when vast numbers of patients were released from mental hospitals without a safety net of treatment, community services, or housing. Cisneros is the former Secretary of the U.S. Department of Housing and Urban Development.

As you read, consider the following questions:
1. What is the greatest threat posed by mentally ill homeless people, in Cisneros's view?
2. What factors make individuals with serious mental illnesses vulnerable to homelessness, as stated by the author?
3. According to the author, what "worst possible combination of events" happened with respect to deinstitutionalization?

Excerpted from "Searching for Home: Mentally Ill Homeless People in America," by Henry G. Cisneros, 1996, as it appeared online at www.huduser.org/publications/txt/essay10.txt. Reprinted by permission of the Urban Institute, Washington, D.C.

On any given night in the United States, an estimated 600,000 people are homeless. Of those, approximately 200,000 suffer from serious mental illness. Unfortunately, these are facts that no longer hold surprise for most Americans. We have grown accustomed to the sight of the wild eyed, dirt-covered man on the corner. We have become used to averting our gaze from the toothless old woman who mutters to herself at the bus stop and wears many layers of clothes even in warm weather. We are no longer as shocked as we were a decade ago at the sight of small children crouched beside their parents, panhandling on some of our busiest streets. . . .

A Snapshot of Mentally Ill Homeless People in America

It is difficult to imagine a more dangerous or more distressing combination of problems to befall any one person than to be homeless and to suffer from a severe mental illness. Yet those who are homeless and mentally ill are often diagnosed with many accompanying disabilities—such as drug addiction, alcoholism, HIV/AIDS, diabetes, and tuberculosis. Mentally ill homeless people tend to be the sickest, the most ragged, and the most difficult people for society to accept. In addition, because rationality itself is compromised by mental illness, they are often the least able to help themselves, either economically or medically, and thus they slide more deeply into danger.

Who are mentally ill homeless persons, and how do they survive? They are among the poorest people in our Nation, earning or receiving in Supplemental Security Income (SSI) and other benefits an average annual income of $4,200. While most would like to work, this population faces some of the highest barriers to employment. It is estimated that one-half of the mentally ill homeless people suffer from drug and alcohol abuse, and many use substances as a method of self-medication. An estimated 4 percent to 14 percent of adults in family shelters have been in a mental hospital.

Because mentally ill homeless men and women are vulnerable to attack, they are often victims of violent crime. Some of the crimes against them are examples of the worst behavior imaginable. But many mentally ill homeless also come into contact with the criminal justice system as offenders, arrested as they engage in such illegal activities as trespassing, petty theft, shoplifting, and prostitution—often crimes of survival under the most desperate of conditions, and a direct result of their mental illness. . . .

A Threat to Themselves

While some individuals are a threat to others, the greatest threat many mentally ill homeless people pose is to themselves. More than once, I have had conversations with men and women in obvious misery and pleaded with them to get a broken leg set or to come in out of the cold, only to have my offers rejected. Unable to comprehend the origin of their pain, and always suspicious of offers of help, these people become vulnerable to freezing to death in winter, having limbs amputated, or dying prematurely from a range of illnesses.

The median age of the homeless has decreased. The average homeless person today is in his or her early to mid-30s. Although 21 percent of homeless persons with mental illnesses at community mental health centers are self-referrals, the majority of homeless clients are referred to the centers by emergency shelters, hospital emergency rooms, police, State psychiatric hospitals, and the criminal justice system.

These individuals suffer from severe mental illnesses such as schizophrenia, mood disorders, severe depression, and personality disorders. Given consistent medical and psychosocial treatment along with stable housing, many of them could again function at a high level. But such stability and consistent care are impossible to achieve when one is homeless. Thus homelessness and mental illness become a vicious circle, one compounding the other in a vortex of suffering for the individual. Unfortunately, without mental health treatment and related support services, it is difficult for mentally ill homeless persons to gain access to, and remain in, permanent housing. Often they face stigma associated with their illness and discrimination by potential landlords or neighbors. All of these factors make individuals with serious mental illnesses extremely vulnerable to homelessness and difficult to help once they become homeless.

The Deinstitutionalization Experiment

The emptying of our public psychiatric hospitals has been the second-largest social experiment in twentieth-century America, exceeded only by the New Deal. The experiment, undertaken upon remarkably little data and a multitude of flawed assumptions, has received virtually no formal evaluation or assessment to ascertain whether it has worked. Once the spring of deinstitutionalization was wound, it just kept going and going and going. And it continues today—disastrously.

It is important to realize the magnitude of this experiment. In 1955 state psychiatric hospitals housed 558,239 seriously mentally ill persons. If the same proportion of Americans were hospitalized today, when the U.S. population is much larger, these hospitals would contain some 900,000 seriously mentally ill individuals. In fact the actual number is less than 70,000, meaning that the net deinstitutionalization amounts to some 830,000 people—more than the population of Boston, Baltimore, or San Francisco. . . .

Many who were deinstitutionalized . . . are worse off than if they had remained in the hospital. They can be found talking to themselves in public streets and parks, living in cardboard boxes or subway tunnels beneath the city in the middle of winter, or escaping the cold in public libraries. They often end up in jail, charged with misdemeanors. Hundreds of thousands of the deinstitutionalized mentally ill have died prematurely from accidents, suicide, or untreated illnesses. All too frequently, the consequences of this failed social experiment have been tragic and fatal.

E. Fuller Torrey, *City Journal*, Summer 1998.

History of the Problem

Contemporary homelessness came to the general public's attention in the late 1970s and early 1980s. Since the most visible members of the "new" homeless population were often disheveled and disoriented, and since it was common knowledge that State mental hospitals had been returning their chronic patients to the community, many people assumed that the rise in homelessness was a result of State deinstitutionalization policies. The true reasons for the rise in homelessness are far more complex. Deinstitutionalization and the inability of some community mental health programs to serve the most severely disabled did play a significant part in creating the problem, but other factors played important roles as well.

Until the late 1950s and early 1960s, most Americans suffering from serious mental illness were long-term residents of State mental hospitals, where all their care was administered under one roof. Then, because of changes in the technology of mental health treatment (in particular, the advent of psychotropic medications), the process of deinstitutionalization began. Along with the depopulation of State hospitals, stricter criteria were implemented for new admissions, and authority for the planning and provision of mental health services was decentralized from the State to local communities.

The Worst Possible Combination of Events

Advocates of deinstitutionalization knew that the asylum was not the best place for the mentally ill. However, deinstitutionalization was intended to be only the first step in a careful shifting of money and responsibility to community mental health centers. What actually happened was the worst possible combination of events: Deinstitutionalization began, but funds for the planning and implementation that were supposed to create responsive community care were cut.

The population shift was sudden and dramatic. Nationally, the census of State mental hospitals was reduced from 560,000 in 1955 to 216,000 in 1974 and to 100,000 in 1989. Many formerly institutionalized patients either died, were eventually moved to nursing homes, or moved in with their families. Others were denied admission to State hospitals because of the stricter admission policies or were admitted for shorter stays. Upon release, they went home to live with their families; were placed in group homes or supervised apartments run by mental health centers; or resided in board-and-care homes, single-room occupancy (SRO) hotels, and other forms of marginal housing. Many mentally ill people were released from institutions without a safety net of assured treatment, supportive services, or appropriate housing.

Because mental health systems are run by States, the rate and timing of deinstitutionalization varied by State. In New York, for example, the depopulation of State hospitals was largely completed by 1978, before the rise in homelessness there became pronounced. In Illinois, the State hospital population dropped from 23,000 in 1971 to 10,000 in 1980.

Patients who were deinstitutionalized or discharged from short-term hospitalization without adequate housing and supportive services were not the only persons to suffer from the lack of community-based resources. The National Institute of Mental Health (NIMH) funded 10 studies to determine the socioeconomic and mental health status and the service needs of homeless people. By 1989 this body of research had established that approximately one-third of the single adult homeless population had a serious mental illness and about one-half of this subgroup had a co-occurring substance-use disorder. NIMH also found that only about one-half of this group had ever been hospitalized for a psychiatric disorder. The lack of an accessible, comprehensive system of community care meant that many who in an earlier era would probably have been institutionalized fell through the social safety net and ended up on the streets.

"Addiction both precipitates and sustains homelessness."

Substance Abuse Is a Cause of Homelessness

San Diego Regional Task Force on the Homeless

Studies have documented that one-third of the homeless population suffers from chronic alcoholism and one-tenth abuse drugs other than alcohol. In the following viewpoint, the San Diego Regional Task Force on the Homeless asserts that substance abuse is often a cause of homelessness because it inhibits a person's ability to work and to maintain family relationships. Furthermore, once homeless, many people use alcohol and drugs as a means of coping with their problems. The San Diego Regional Task Force is a partnership of public agencies, private groups, and homeless advocates whose goal is to end homelessness in San Diego County.

As you read, consider the following questions:

1. As cited by the author, what percentage of urban homeless adults suffer from alcoholism, drug addiction, mental illness, or some combination of the three?
2. What is the profile of an alcoholic homeless person, as stated by the San Diego Regional Task Force?
3. What is the impact of alcoholism on homeless people, according to the author?

Excerpted from "Substance Abuse and Homelessness," a publication of the San Diego (California) Regional Task Force on the Homeless, as it appeared online at www.co.san-diego.ca.us/rtfh/alcohol.html (2000). Reprinted with permission.

Significant segments of the urban homeless population have a history or a practice of substance abuse. . . . This is not a new phenomenon—alcoholics have been well represented among the ranks of the homeless for nearly a century.

Based on multiple studies completed in the [1990s], at least a third of the adult homeless population suffers from chronic alcoholism. A smaller portion, approximately 10 percent, of homeless persons have chronic involvement with drugs other than alcohol. In *A Nation in Denial*, Alice S. Baum and Donald W. Burnes estimate that 65 to 80 percent of all (urban) homeless adults suffer from chronic alcoholism, drug addiction, mental illness, or some combination of the three, often complicated by serious medical problems.

The Prevalence of Homeless Substance Abusers

Lack of uniform definitions of alcohol, drug, and mental health problems and variances in methodology make it difficult to generalize findings from the many studies on the prevalence of homeless substance abusers. The ratios cited above are the median estimates of prevalence.

Based on the estimate that half of homeless adults abuse substances, there may be 2,900 to 3,000 homeless adults in [San Diego] County actively abusing or withdrawing from alcohol or drugs, or both.

Approximately one third of the adult urban homeless population suffers from alcohol abuse. This suggests that there may be 1,900 to 2,000 adult urban homeless persons in San Diego County who abuse alcohol. Forty percent of the adult homeless population has had problems with alcohol at some point in their lives. In San Diego County, this represents about 2,300 to 2,400 homeless persons.

Another 600 or so may abuse drugs other than alcohol. Prevalence rates are highest among minority men, followed by African-American women and white men. In general, substance problems are less prevalent among homeless women than among homeless men. The majority of homeless men who abuse drugs are in their late teens and twenties.

Based on the estimate that 65 to 80 percent of all homeless adults suffer from chronic alcoholism, drug addiction, severe mental illness, or some combination of the three, there are 3,800 to 4,700 homeless persons with one or more of these conditions. Half of the severely mentally ill homeless persons in San Diego County are believed to abuse drugs and/or alcohol (persons often referred to as "dually diagnosed"). Substance abuse is both a cause and result of homelessness for the mentally ill. Furthermore, mentally ill homeless persons commonly use illegal drugs or alcohol as a substitute for medication. (A third of severely mentally ill homeless persons are believed to have no contact with mental health professionals.) . . .

Alcohol Abuse

The profile of an alcoholic homeless person generally mirrors the stereotype of homelessness. He (less often, she) tends to be older, has fewer ties to friends or family members, has probably been married in the past, is less transient than other homeless people, and is generally identified as "chronically homeless."

Yet, homeless people with alcohol abuse problems are becoming a more diverse group than the traditional stereotype of the older, white male alcoholic. Youth, minorities, women, poly-drug users, mentally ill persons, and people with less education and fewer vocational skills now comprise more of the homeless population with alcohol problems.

The public perception that most homeless people are alcoholics or drug addicts may stem from the visibility of homeless people drinking, or behaving in an intoxicated manner. Such individuals easily attract the public's attention, while homeless persons who do not drink or use drugs are often unseen.

While community reaction is harsh on the chronically inebriated, the public generally acknowledges that alcoholism is an addictive disease in which the victim has become physically and psychologically dependent on alcohol.

Drug Abuse

Drug use among the homeless population is more concentrated than it is in the general population. Homeless users are also more likely to report choosing "hard drugs," particularly rock cocaine and heroin. Also, homeless drug users tend to be younger and are more likely to be African-American or Hispanic.

There have also been recent increases in the number of homeless, crack-dependent women with children. Some suggest that the arrival of crack cocaine in the mid-1980s partially explains the increase of persons who have moved from precarious living accommodations to the streets.

Street Children and Substance Use

• The percentage of substance users among street children varies greatly depending on the region, availability of substances, gender, age, and circumstances of the children. Studies have found that between 25% and 90% of street children use substances of one kind or another.

• Most street children have virtually no access to health care and community services. As a result, continued substance use among street children usually has serious health and social consequences. In South Africa, for example, as many as 9 out of 10 street children are thought to be dependent on glue.

• The age of initial substance use among street children is very young—as young as five years of age. In Colombia and Bolivia, 8-year-old children have been reported dealing in and smoking basuco cigarettes, a low grade by-product of cocaine laced with kerosene and sulphuric acid.

World Health Organization, "Substance Use Among Street Children and Other Children and Youth in Especially Difficult Circumstances," March 1997.

The needs of this population are greater than that without substance abuse problems. Homeless persons with substance abuse problems are at higher risk for HIV infection and are more likely to have serious health problems and severe mental illness, to be arrested, to be victimized on the streets, and to suffer an early death. Not surprisingly, alcohol and drug abuse are frequently cited as a major obstacle to ending an individual's homelessness.

There is a clear relationship between chronic homelessness and substance abuse in the United States. Addiction both precipitates and sustains homelessness. It also inhibits one's ability to work and destroys families and other social relationships. Consequently, once an abuser loses his or her source of income and housing, friends or family may be unwilling to offer assistance. In an increasingly competitive affordable housing market, drug and alcohol abusers are the last to qualify for housing benefits and thus end up on the streets more frequently than the rest of the low-income population. Additionally, new welfare and Social Security Disability income regulations concerning alcohol and drug abusers severely limit and, in most cases, eliminate this group's eligibility for such assistance.

In addition to persons who become homeless through their own drug addiction, many men, women, and children are displaced from their homes due to a drug-addicted parent or provider.

Substance abuse may also begin after an individual has become homeless, due to the fact that both street life and skid row subculture encourage consumption of alcohol and other drugs. For many homeless persons, drinking or other drug use provides a means to get through the day. Homeless people with mental health problems may also use drugs or alcohol in place of prescription medication in order to cope with their afflictions. . . .

The Immediate and Long-Term
Needs of Homeless Substance Abusers

The impact of alcoholism is more severe for homeless persons than the general population, as measured by physiological and behavioral symptoms of the disease. These may include blackouts, delirium tremens, early morning drinking, and adverse social consequences such as drinking-related arrests, family dissolutions, and loss of jobs.

Housing programs often reject substance abusers. The sobriety requirements for such programs are difficult to meet if individuals cannot access treatment independently or if local communities do not have programs for those dually diagnosed with mental illness and substance abuse problems.

Programs designed specifically for those who are dually diagnosed are important. Some alcohol programs emphasize completely drug-free environments in contrast to mental health programs that rely on medication to stabilize their clients. Some alcohol programs with a strong self-help orientation are reluctant to accept mental health services with strong clinical and professional orientations, and vice versa.

It is very difficult for an individual to stay sober without stable economic support, whether it is a job or public entitlement. It is also difficult to achieve and maintain sobriety without a place to live. And there is little chance that a person can remain sober without medical care for other physical or mental disabilities.

"[One] study found that 50% of homeless women and children were fleeing abuse."

Domestic Violence Contributes to Homelessness

National Coalition for the Homeless

The National Coalition for the Homeless (NCH), an organization whose mission is to end homelessness through public education, policy advocacy, and grassroots organizing, claims in the subsequent viewpoint that domestic violence is often the cause of homelessness among women and children. According to multiple research studies, writes NCH, the most common reason women enter a homeless shelter is to flee an abusive relationship.

As you read, consider the following questions:

1. How many cities surveyed by the U.S. Conference of Mayors identified domestic violence as a primary cause of homelessness, as stated by the author?
2. According to NCH, what percentage of homeless women in Minnesota cite abuse as one of their main reasons for leaving housing?
3. What is the necessary first step in meeting the needs of women fleeing domestic violence, in the author's view?

Reprinted from "Domestic Violence and Homelessness," Fact Sheet #8 (April 1999), of the National Coalition for the Homeless, found at www.nch.ari.net/domestic.html. Used with permission.

When a woman leaves an abusive relationship, she often has nowhere to go. This is particularly true of women with few resources. Lack of affordable housing and long waiting lists for assisted housing mean that many women and their children are forced to choose between abuse at home or the streets. Moreover, shelters are frequently filled to capacity and must turn away battered women and their children. An estimated 32% of requests for shelter by homeless families were denied in 1998 due to lack of resources.

Domestic Violence as a Contributing Factor to Homelessness

Many studies demonstrate the contribution of domestic violence to homelessness, particularly among families with children. A 1990 Ford Foundation study found that 50% of homeless women and children were fleeing abuse. More recently, in a study of 777 homeless parents (the majority of whom were mothers) in ten U.S. cities, 22% said they had left their last place of residence because of domestic violence. In addition, 46% of cities surveyed by the U.S. Conference of Mayors identified domestic violence as a primary cause of homelessness. State and local studies also demonstrate the impact of domestic violence on homelessness:

- In Minnesota, the most common reason for women to enter a shelter is domestic violence. Approximately one in five women (19%) surveyed indicated that one of the main reasons for leaving housing was to flee abuse; 24% of women surveyed were homeless, at least in part, because of a previous abuse experience.
- In Missouri, 18% of the sheltered homeless population are victims of domestic violence.
- A 1995 survey of homeless adults in Michigan found that physical abuse/being afraid of someone was most frequently cited as the main cause of homelessness.
- Shelter providers in Virginia report that 35% of their clients are homeless because of family violence. This same survey found that more than 2,000 women seeking shelter from domestic violence facilities were turned away.

Policy Issues

Shelters provide immediate safety to battered women and their children and help women gain control over their lives. The provision of safe emergency shelter is thus a necessary first step in meeting the needs of women fleeing domestic violence.

A sizable portion of the welfare population experiences domestic violence at any given time; thus, without significant housing support, many welfare recipients are at risk of

Research on Domestic Violence and Homelessness

A review of the literature suggests that lifetime prevalence rates of physical and sexual assaults in studies of homeless women are particularly high. Physical and sexual abuse are often the subtext in stories of women's homelessness. For example, in a study of 426 homeless and poor housed mothers, Brown & Bassuk, (1997) findings indicated that over 60% of the total sample experienced severe physical assault by an intimate male partner during adulthood, nearly a third (32.4%) had been the target of severe violence by their current or most recent partner.

In a small sample of homeless women, Redmond and Brackmann (1990) found that 50% of the homeless women they interviewed had been physically assaulted as children, 33% reported child sexual molestation, and 33% reported experiencing violence with their most recent adult partner.

An in-depth interview with 141 women at a Manhattan shelter, D'Ercole and Struening (1990) yielded prevalence estimates of 31% for child sexual molestation and 63% for violence by an adult male partner.

The only study of homeless mothers that used comprehensive measures in focusing on family violence, found that 60% of the homeless mothers reported child physical abuse, 42% reported sexual molestation, and 65% reported physical assault by their most recent adult partner (Goodman, 1991).

Findings from a study conducted by Breton & Bunston (1992), on physical and sexual violence in the lives of homeless women, revealed that 85.7% of the homeless women in their sample reported being physically assaulted by a partner, 52.4% reported being sexually assaulted, and 38.1% reported experiencing both types of violence by adult partners.

Jane Tyschenko, "Domestic Violence as a Factor in Women's Homelessness." Available at www.uic.edu/classes/socw/socw517/homelesstyschenko.htm.

homelessness or continued violence. In states that have looked at domestic violence and welfare receipt, most report that approximately 50–60% of current recipients say that they have experienced violence from a current or former male partner. In the absence of cash assistance, women who experience domestic violence may be at increased risk of homelessness or compelled to live with a former or current abuser in order to prevent homelessness. Welfare programs must make every effort to assist victims of domestic violence and to recognize the tremendous barrier to employment that domestic violence presents.

Long-term efforts to address homelessness must include increasing the supply of affordable housing, ensuring adequate wages and income supports, and providing necessary supportive services.

Periodical Bibliography

The following articles have been selected to supplement the diverse views presented in this chapter. Addresses are provided for periodicals not indexed in the *Readers' Guide to Periodical Literature*, the *Alternative Press Index*, the *Social Sciences Index*, or the *Index to Legal Periodicals and Books*.

America	"Crisis on Low-Income Rental Housing," July 4, 1998.
Camille Colatosti	"Squandering the Future: A Nation of Children Living in Poverty," *Witness*, April 1999. Available from 7000 Michigan Ave., Detroit, MI 48210-2872 or at www.thewitness.org.
Florence Isaacs	"Mean Streets," *Parents*, September 1997.
Bob Levin	"The Kids Who Make It in from the Cold," *Maclean's*, December 21, 1998.
John Mulligan	"Shopping Cart Soldiers," *American Legion*, October 1998. Available from the American Legion, 5561 W. 74th St., Indianapolis, IN 46268.
National Coalition for the Homeless	"The Impact of Welfare Reform on Homelessness," *Safety Network*, May/June 1998. Available at http://nch.ari.net/sn/1998/may/impact.html.
E. Fuller Torrey	"Let's Stop Being Nutty About the Mentally Ill," *City Journal*, Summer 1998. Available at www.city-journal.org/html/7_3_a2.html.

CHAPTER 3

What Housing Options Would Benefit the Homeless?

Chapter Preface

In 1965, as part of President Lyndon B. Johnson's War on Poverty, the Department of Housing and Urban Development (HUD) was established as a federal agency responsible for addressing America's housing needs. In the agency's own words, its official mission is to provide "a decent, safe, and sanitary home and suitable living environment for every American."

Since its inception, one of HUD's primary goals has been to develop affordable housing options for the nation's poor, through programs such as public housing and rent subsidies. HUD's efforts to combat homelessness, however, did not begin until 1987, when the Stewart B. McKinney Homelessness Assistance Act became the first significant piece of federal legislation to deal with homelessness.

The McKinney Act funds four major programs intended to help the homeless find housing and achieve self-sufficiency: 1) the Supportive Housing Program, which funds housing and services that enable homeless people to live independently; 2) Shelter Plus Care, which provides rental assistance to homeless people with disabilities and their families; 3) the Single Room Occupancy Program, which rehabilitates buildings with single-room dwellings and makes payments to landlords for the homeless people who rent the rehabilitated units; and 4) Emergency Shelter Grants, which fund the conversion of buildings into homeless shelters.

In recent years, though, Congress has reduced funding of McKinney programs—a move that has provoked vocal criticism from many homeless advocates, who argue that funding cuts severely inhibit the programs' effectiveness. However, some conservative politicians favor the elimination of government programs such as those developed under the McKinney Act, claiming that private organizations and local governments are more efficient at helping the homeless. Authors in the subsequent chapter discuss the advantages and disadvantages of federal housing programs and propose a variety of housing options for low-income and homeless individuals.

"There is now an urgent need to strengthen federal efforts to assure adequate supplies of decent, safe, and affordable housing for America's struggling families."

The Federal Government Should Work to Provide Affordable Housing

Andrew Cuomo

In the following viewpoint, Andrew Cuomo, then U.S. Secretary of Housing and Urban Development, argues that the government should play a strong role in providing affordable housing for low-income families, most of whom are priced out of today's competitive rental market. Federal housing policies such as rent vouchers, public housing programs, and tax incentives for home ownership allow the poor to meet their housing needs, thus preventing homelessness.

Editor's Note: The following viewpoint is excerpted from testimony given to the U.S. Senate Committee on Appropriations, Subcommittee on Veteran Affairs, Housing and Urban Development, and Independent Agencies.

As you read, consider the following questions:
1. What are the three main findings of the HUD's report on rental housing, as stated by Cuomo?
2. According to the author, what is at the core of HUD's mission?
3. What percentage of public housing residents are satisfied or very satisfied with their housing, as cited by the author?

Excerpted from Andrew Cuomo's testimony before the U.S. Senate Committee on Appropriations, Subcommittee on VA, HUD, and Independent Agencies, March 30, 2000.

M r. Chairman, I believe that this year we are at a cross-roads. This year, the first year of the new millennium, we must make a choice. That choice is whether we build on our success and take a bold step towards once and for all addressing our nation's affordable housing needs. This year we have an extraordinary opportunity to set this nation on a new course, so that when the historians write the history of housing in this century, they will be able to say that this was truly the year we made good on the goal of a "decent, safe and affordable home for every American family."

Facing a Crisis

And there should be no doubt that we are facing a crisis. It is a term that I do not use lightly. The evidence, unfortunately, is clear. It is impossible to open the newspaper today without reading reports describing the problem in communities in virtually every part of the country. Almost every day there are articles about rising rents and the lack of affordable housing—both in big cities like San Francisco, Los Angeles, Dallas, Miami and New York, as well as in smaller and medium-sized cities like Rochester, Norfolk, and Sacramento.

It is a cruel irony that while most communities are doing very well in this booming economy, the better they are doing the more acute their shortage of affordable housing. Those that are doing the best are often also facing the worst shortages. The stronger the economy, the stronger the upward pressure on rents. Even some of America's strongest regions for business are literally being "priced out" of housing by their success. In Silicon Valley, the leading companies driving the global information age have identified affordable housing as their number one backyard concern.

[The U.S. Department of Housing and Urban Development's (HUD)] new worst case housing needs report . . . gives us a nation-wide picture that confirms these local reports. . . . It is entitled *Rental Housing Assistance—The Worsening Crisis*. It's the most in-depth, comprehensive and respected analysis of rental housing in the United States.

There are a number of dramatic findings in this report. I would like to highlight three of them today. The first, and most important, is that, despite the booming economy, the number of families with worst case housing needs has increased to 5.4 million—an all-time high. Since the last worst case housing needs report was released [in 1998], the number of families with worst case needs has increased by 4%, twice the rate of growth for the U.S. population.

Households with Worst Case Needs

Households with worst case needs are defined as unassisted renters with incomes below 50 percent of the local median, who pay more than half of their income for rent or live in severely substandard housing.

Even more compelling than the record number of worst case needs is the increase that we've seen over the past decade. There are now 600,000 more households with worst case housing needs than there were in 1991 when the current economic recovery began—a rate of increase that is almost twice as fast as overall household growth.

A second important finding of this report is that families with worst case needs are working harder than ever. While you would expect that the poorest families also have the worst case needs, the fact is that the number of people who work full-time and have worst case housing needs increased by 28% from 1991 to 1997—a rate of growth that is almost twice as fast as the rate for all other low-income renters. People used to think that if you were willing to work hard, things would take care of themselves. You would be able to afford housing and take care of your family. But that, unfortunately, is not always the case any more.

The third finding I want to highlight is that low-income Americans who live in the suburbs, not the cities, are more likely to have worst case needs than elsewhere. It disproves the myth that the affordable housing shortage in this country is an urban problem. It's the suburbs where you're seeing the largest drop-off in the number of affordable housing units available. In fact, over one third of all worst case households live in the suburbs.

A Clear and Compelling Case for Federal Support

These findings make a clear and compelling case for greater federal attention to our nation's housing needs. With this

Committee's support and through bipartisan cooperation, we have broken the gridlock on affordable housing, when Congress approved new housing vouchers in each of the past two years—60,000 last year and 50,000 the year before.

With worst case needs at record levels, there is now an urgent need to strengthen federal efforts to assure adequate supplies of decent, safe, and affordable housing for America's struggling families.

That is the need that our FY [fiscal year] 2001 budget proposals address, Mr. Chairman. That is why we have requested continued support from Congress for incremental housing vouchers to help meet the housing needs of low-income families struggling with rising rents.

And that is why President [Clinton] has asked for an overall $6 billion increase over last year's enacted level. It reflects his belief that we must squarely address this rental housing crisis, that we must address the needs of those people and places left behind in this new economy, that we must help working families move closer to job opportunities—and that HUD now has the strength to address these challenges effectively and responsibly.

HUD Can Address the Nation's Housing Crisis

A few years ago, some would have argued that while the need was there, HUD did not have the capacity to address it. I am pleased to tell you that that is no longer the case. By virtually any measure, and according to every independent expert, HUD today not only has the capacity, but is better positioned than ever to help communities take on the challenges of the 21st century.

This year's budget proposal is a direct outcome of the management reforms we have put in place over the past three years. I am convinced that we now have the tools, the resources, and the capacity to wisely and responsibly spend the funds we have requested.

Our management reforms have succeeded in transforming HUD into an agency that puts communities first. Fighting fraud, waste, and abuse, our Public Trust Officers are cracking down on those who misuse taxpayer dollars. Renewing our commitment to first-class customer service, our Community Builders are connecting people to the full range of HUD resources. As a result, HUD today is back in business—back in the housing business, in the economic development business, and in the community empowerment business. . . .

At the core of HUD's mission is the charge to provide housing that is decent, safe and, affordable to all. As I stated earlier, it is actually becoming more and more difficult for low-income American families to afford a decent place to live. Rents have soared in many regions with strong economies. Worst case housing needs have reached an all-time high of 5.4 million households, growing especially fast among working families. As a result, there is a greater need than ever for HUD's programs.

HUD's Housing Programs

Our FY 2001 initiatives build on recent efforts to reform and restore public trust in HUD's housing programs. Historic legislation created the Mark-to-Market program, which preserves project-based Section 8 housing while bringing costs in line with the private market. We have cracked down on program abuses. Our Real Estate Assessment Center is on track towards meeting our goal of inspecting, for the first time, all 40,000 properties in HUD's inventory of public housing and multifamily insured or assisted housing. And more than 600 troubled properties have been referred to the new Enforcement Center, with 45% of the cases resolved and revenues from fines imposed in FY 99 up five times over the previous year.

Section 8 renewals and incremental vouchers. HUD is requesting $13.0 billion in new budget authority to renew existing Section 8 contracts, covering 2.6 million rental units. In addition, we are requesting $690 million for 120,000 new vouchers, the largest increase since 1981. In 1998, HUD got back into the housing business with 50,000 new vouchers focused on families moving from welfare to work. We topped that last year with 60,000. With this year's request, we are taking the next step. These new vouchers will be targeted as follows: One half, or 60,000, will be "Fair Share" vouchers, to be used by public housing authorities to reduce their waiting lists; 32,000 will be targeted to those moving from welfare to work; 18,000 will be for homeless persons; and 10,000 will stimulate new housing production that will be affordable to extremely low-income individuals.

New housing production vouchers. Our proposal for new vouchers includes the first Section 8 housing production vouchers in 17 years. For decades, national housing policy has shifted back and forth between production-oriented programs (that focus on expanding the supply of affordable housing) and income-based initiatives (that provide cash assistance to enable lower-income families to afford rental housing). As we enter the 21st century, it is clear that both approaches are needed if America is to realize the goal of decent housing for all. We are proposing 10,000 housing production vouchers that, in tandem with the Low Income Housing Tax Credit and FHA insurance, will leverage 40,000 total units (subsidized and unsubsidized).

Ben Sargent. Copyright © 1998 Austin American Statesman. Reprinted by permission of Universal Press Syndicate. All rights reserved.

Public housing. In 1998, Congress enacted landmark bipartisan public housing legislation, that brought working families into public housing without sacrificing our historic commitment to low-income and very low-income persons. Through our new physical inspections system, we have now inspected every property in public housing—and the results are in: 84% of all public housing properties are in sound or excellent condition, and customer satisfaction surveys show that 75% of all public housing residents are satisfied or very satisfied with their housing. That's a customer satisfaction rating that beats the banking, the utility, and the retail industries.

Transforming Public Housing

HUD's FY 2001 budget continues our efforts to transform public housing. We are requesting a $54 million increase in public housing operating funds, to almost $3.2 billion, or 100% of PFS. We also are proposing almost $2.96 billion for the Capital Fund to help public housing authorities modernize or rehabilitate public housing units that are in need of significant repairs or replacement, an increase of $86 million over the FY 2000 enacted level.

Finally, we are requesting $625 million for HOPE VI, which is revolutionizing public housing by replacing obsolete high rises or barracks-style projects with new, mixed-income, mixed-use livable communities and housing vouchers. Through 2000, the program is expected to approve the demolition of 100,000 units. By 2003, our goal is to approve 145,000 units for replacement with hard units or with vouchers.

Home Investment Partnerships Program (HOME). Since it was created ten years ago, the HOME program has become a proven housing rehabilitation and production tool in both urban and rural America. We are requesting $1.65 billion, a $50 million increase over last year's level. This will provide approximately 103,000 units of affordable housing for both owners and renters through a combination of new construction, rehabilitation, acquisition and tenant-based assistance.

Homeownership. Over the past three years we have done more than ever to bring homeownership to underserved markets. I'm proud of the record homeownership rate of 66.8%; but the real success is what we've done to close the gap for minorities, first time buyers, younger couples, residents of cities. We have increased the affordable housing goals of the GSEs from 42% to 50%. Fifty percent of their total purchases must aid low- and moderate-income Americans. With higher FHA loan limits enacted by Congress, in FY 1999 we boosted FHA loans to a record 1.3 million—40% of which were to minority buyers. Automated underwriting has dramatically reduced underwriting times for applicants. And the process for disposition of foreclosed properties has been improved substantially. . . .

Homelessness and Special Needs. Over the past seven years [prior to 2000], we have made significant progress on homelessness in America. When I first came to HUD, the entire federal government had been spending about the same as just the state of New York on homeless assistance. Since then, we've more than doubled the amount of federal homeless assistance.

But this is about more than just the dollars and cents. It is about a new, comprehensive approach, the Continuum of Care, that we've put in place—a holistic approach aimed at moving people into permanent housing and self-sufficiency. According to a study by Columbia University, we are now serving 14 times more people than we were in 1993. This progress was recognized when last year the Continuum won the prestigious Innovations in Government Award from Harvard University and the Ford Foundation.

By all measures, the Continuum of Care is working. Accordingly, for FY 2001, we are proposing $1.2 billion for homeless assistance, an increase of $180 million. We also propose to shift the source of Rinds for Shelter Plus Care contract renewals to the Section 8 Housing Certificate Fund, creating additional savings for localities and homeless service providers. This increase, plus 18,000 new rental vouchers to create permanent housing solutions, will address the housing needs of the most vulnerable Americans—those making a transition from the streets back into homes and community life.

| "*[The] network of privately built and maintained neighborhoods suggests that massive government spending is not needed to help those of low and moderate income find good housing.*"

The Federal Government Should Not Work to Provide Affordable Housing

Howard Husock

Howard Husock maintains in the subsequent viewpoint that the federal government should allocate little or no money to fund low-income housing. According to Husock, public housing, rent vouchers, and other programs that depend on federal subsidies destroy recipients' incentives to work harder and improve their economic position. Private housing initiatives have proven to be far more effective than costly government programs at helping low-income families find affordable housing. Husock is the director of the Case Study Program at Harvard University's John F. Kennedy School of Government.

As you read, consider the following questions:

1. In what way is the "housing ladder" a social system, as stated by Husock?
2. What is the main disadvantage of housing vouchers, according to the author?
3. In the author's view, what psychological transition must society make regarding low-income housing?

Reprinted from "Broken Ladder: Government Thwarts Affordable Housing," by Howard Husock, *Policy Review*, March/April 1997, by permission of the Heritage Foundation.

From all appearances, federal policy on affordable housing is facing its most searching reassessment in decades. As housing policy comes up for reauthorization in Congress, the decades-old approach of housing low-income tenants in massive housing projects has few defenders in Washington. The Clinton administration seems to favor the demolition of some of the notorious projects, relocating some of their former tenants in newer, largely mixed-income units, and assisting others with vouchers to subsidize their rental of housing in the private market. On the Republican side, Rick Lazio, the chairman of the housing and community opportunity subcommittee, has gone so far as to suggest repealing the National Housing Act of 1937, the basis for all current federal housing programs. In addition, he has advocated potential time limits for public-housing tenants and tougher oversight of corrupt housing authorities.

None of these proposals, however, have challenged the intellectual basis of current housing policy. Both sides have essentially proposed marginal changes intended mainly to ameliorate the worst aspects of public and subsidized housing. Unfortunately, the changes rest on dubious assumptions— chief among them that the problems with our housing policy have stemmed from its implementation rather than its very conception. We are told that public housing might work if only it did not take the form of high-rises and serve mainly the very poor, that low-income housing subsidies should certainly work if only they were provided in the form of vouchers that will open up the private housing market to those in need. But since these proposed reforms ignore the powerful social dynamics that shape neighborhoods, we are in danger of lurching toward a new generation of policy mistakes.

A Way Out of Housing Policy Problems

There is another way out of our housing policy problems. Throughout the country, we see innovative models of housing that work and, in most instances, are neither politically divisive nor dependent on government subsidies. This network of privately built and maintained neighborhoods suggests that massive government spending is not needed to help those of low and moderate income find good housing.

The key to understanding what works is a concept called the housing ladder: the idea that neighborhoods and the types of homes in them shape the way we organize our society and its social structure. Public officials who understand the housing ladder can help citizens of any income secure good homes and neighborhoods. If we understand its rules, its social dynamics, government can help extend housing opportunities through use of the market and, at most, limited subsidies.

In 1979, geographer Phillip Rees found that socioeconomic status is a universal sorting principle in American cities. People of similar incomes and educational backgrounds overwhelmingly choose to live together. The result: Most neighborhoods comprise relatively similar lots and types of housing. Each type of neighborhood is linked roughly to an income group. Each type of neighborhood represents a rung on the housing ladder.

But the housing ladder is not just a system of physical structures; it's also a social system. Families strive to improve their economic position—to climb to a higher rung. A bigger and better house in a more affluent neighborhood is one of the rewards that market economies bestow upon individuals. Unlike other consumer goods, the value of one's house is, in part, determined by the condition of one's neighborhood. Keeping a neighborhood safe and property values high is a common enterprise that helps hold communities together. Residents may, for example, work hard to forestall neighborhood deterioration and so avoid falling to a lower rung.

Residents fashion the civil society of their neighborhoods through myriad activities—organizing crime patrols, volunteering at a local school, or simply doing favors for neighbors—that make an area a better place to live. Every day, citizens join in this confidence-building enterprise to reassure each other that their neighborhood will remain attractive to new buyers, will remain a good place to live and increase in value, and may provide the wherewithal to move up to a more expensive neighborhood.

In general, housing policy is a local matter. Every municipality, every residential neighborhood, plays a role. How a community designs its zoning and building codes both reflects and shapes its sense of where it fits within the housing ladder. Properly maintained, the housing ladder provides a full range of privately owned housing options, from cheap single rooms with shared baths to mansions on large plots. Such an array of choices motivates residents of all incomes to maintain their homes and communities and strive to ascend the ladder to better accommodations. This dynamic is key to preserving the social fabric that holds all healthy communities together. It can be awkward to acknowledge that Americans group themselves on the basis of income and education (which are, of course, related). But such are the unwritten rules of the housing ladder, and we ignore them at our peril.

A Vexing Problem

The housing ladder poses a vexing problem. At the lowest rungs, private builders and property owners may erect structures that society believes are not fit for habitation. Shacks, urban shanties, windowless tenements, and converted garages and cellars scandalize reformers and legislators. Historically, government's pursuit of decent housing for all has been based on the belief that substandard housing is not simply smaller and less ornate than middle-class housing, but can deprive its inhabitants of life opportunities and threaten their health and safety.

But when policies to improve housing conditions for the poor ignore the rules of the housing ladder, they inevitably fail. Regulations that raise living conditions also raise construction and maintenance costs, thereby reducing the supply of cheap housing. Costly subsidies for housing based on financial need destroys the incentives of the recipients to save money and to maintain the condition of their environment.

The failure of public housing is commonly attributed to the poor management and high-rise architecture of housing projects and their subsidized successors. But its main flaw is that it deprives poor families of the kind of social fabric that wards off lawlessness and decay. Such accommodations are often physically equal to those for which persons of greater means might pay. But they undermine the incentives to maintain the housing stock that undergird communities.

$384 Billion Down the Drain

Since 1962, we have spent $384 billion through the Department of Housing and Urban Development (HUD) and its federal predecessors. Yet physical maintenance of housing projects is abysmal: A 1988 study estimated that fixing up the nation's public-housing stock, which houses one-third of the 4 million families receiving housing assistance, would cost at least $30 billion. Social maladies—crime, drug abuse, pregnancy among unwed teenagers—are concentrated in, and sometimes exacerbated by, public housing. A 1989 HUD study found that fewer than 10 percent of housing-project families with children are headed by a married couple. Once in the projects, many single-parent families remain, and remain on public assistance.

Where Government Housing Subsidies Go

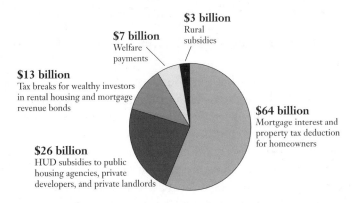

$3 billion
Rural subsidies

$7 billion
Welfare payments

$13 billion
Tax breaks for wealthy investors in rental housing and mortgage revenue bonds

$26 billion
HUD subsidies to public housing agencies, private developers, and private landlords

$64 billion
Mortgage interest and property tax deduction for homeowners

Pentagon subsidies to house military personnel, about $10 billion annually, are not included here.

Source: *American Prospect*, Summer 1995.

In contrast, poor owners and so-called tenement landlords (owners of small, multifamily buildings) seeking home improvements once contributed their own time and hired neighborhood tradesmen. Public housing did away with this type of informal system. Suddenly a public bureaucracy, with its bidding rules and standardized procedures, arranges all repairs. The result has been the decline both of physical structures and the civil society of poorer neighborhoods.

Not only does public housing weaken the social structure within, but the lure of larger, less expensive accommodations than families could otherwise afford draws families out of surrounding neighborhoods and thereby undermines them. Denied their supply of low-income tenants, the fragile private housing market in poor neighborhoods may suffer foreclosures and abandonment.

Public housing also rewards those who have not worked and sacrificed to gain their accommodations; their need alone is considered qualification enough. Absent subsidies, the price of housing serves as a way to separate those among the poor with good work habits and strong family bonds from those who lack them. Public housing deprives low-income citizens who are ambitious and self-sacrificing of an incentive to distance themselves from those who are not. In so doing, it inhibits the formation of strong communities on the lower rungs of upward mobility.

Alternative Policies That Offer No Improvement

It can be argued, of course, that we have learned from our mistakes in public housing. But we have ignored the true lessons from this failure. As a result, we've developed alternative policies that offer no significant improvement.

Housing vouchers. Housing vouchers, which now account for a third of the nearly $8 billion spent annually in federal housing subsidies, offer a dangerous, perverse incentive. In effect, they offer tenants a chance to move to higher-income, or slightly less poor, neighborhoods without having raised their own incomes. By rewarding need, not achievement, vouchers send the wrong message to those they subsidize and threaten to introduce social problems to the neighborhoods into which voucher-holders move.

Subsidized construction. Even as our cities bristle with the remains of previous utopian housing visions, we have embarked on a vast new round of subsidized housing construction—one in which government's role is indirect but crucial. This new approach still produces subsidized rental complexes, but relies on nonprofit community management groups to oversee them. Its premise is that the flaw of public housing has been poor management by housing authorities. Nonprofit groups, it is thought, will do better.

The National Congress for Community Economic Development has estimated that there are more than 2,000 nonprofit, community-based development organizations (CBDOs) in the United States. Most of them—about 88 percent—help create so-called affordable housing: subsidized units for those of lower income. Between 1987 and 1991, these organizations alone produced at least 87,000 housing units, many of them renovations of older apartment buildings in poor neighborhoods. In doing so, they have relied mainly on federal support. Community-based development organizations depend largely on federal tax credits and housing subsidies. But some of the same problems that have dogged public housing, including maintenance problems, are already developing in these new projects.

A common belief among public-housing advocates is that private ownership and production of housing will inevitably ill serve those of modest means. There is good reason to question this core belief. For much of this century, housing reformers have tried to eliminate overcrowded, unsafe, and unhealthy conditions deemed intolerable in a wealthy and compassionate society. In so doing, they have also removed many of the lowest rungs of the housing ladder. The utterly predictable reduction in the supply of affordable housing has in turn been used to justify massive government subsidies.

Models of Private Housing

It is time to rediscover the virtues of privately owned low- and moderate-income housing. What follows are descriptions of initiatives in cities across the United States that help create those rungs on the housing ladder needed to generate good, safe neighborhoods and offer social and economic upward mobility. Each initiative represents its own rung on the ladder. They have been chosen not as programs to be slavishly imitated, but as examples of how a housing policy might take shape when it is based on less regulation, less subsidy, and more attention to the social forces at work in neighborhoods.

San Diego's SRO housing. After World War II, urban renewal programs to raise housing standards decimated the supply of single-room-occupancy (SRO) units. Between 1974 and 1983, 896,000 housing units in the United States renting for less than $200 a month, many of them single-room units, were demolished.

San Diego, California, was no exception. Downtown redevelopment led to significant demolition or conversion of the city's SRO stock, which declined 25 percent from 1976 to 1985. In recent years, however, more than 2,700 new or renovated, privately owned, single-room units have come into the market, most built and run without public subsidy. For this we can thank subtle but crucial regulatory changes that reduced construction costs enough to allow SRO developers to keep rents in line with their low-income market.

To lower costs for private developers of SRO housing, city agencies permitted new SRO hotels in inexpensive commercial zones on the fringe of downtown; exempted SROs from complex zoning and planning reviews; secured state permission to reduce the minimum room size for single-room units and allow rooms to have partial baths and shared showers; allowed builders to satisfy building codes in the cheapest way consistent with safety; and waived regulations for minimum parking, sewer capacity, and other requirements on a case-by-case basis.

Baltimore's minimal rehab model. The decline of inner-city neighborhoods after World War II prompted the federal government to subsidize the interior renovation of buildings in older neighborhoods through so-called gut rehabs. The costs of renovation were higher than the rent rolls in poor neighborhoods could ever support. To draw private owners and managers into the low-income housing business, therefore, the government provided subsidized mortgages for owners and rental subsidies for tenants.

Because much of their rent is paid for by the government, tenants lack leverage to demand proper upkeep and maintenance. Owners, in turn, have neither opportunity nor incentive to screen tenants for ability to pay rent and stay out of trouble. Such renovations are extremely expensive and disrupt the housing ladder. They minimize the incentive to move up, because residents are unlikely to acquire with their own income accommodations equal to what they've gained through subsidy.

A small project called City Homes, Inc., in Baltimore, has a different approach: reduce rents and satisfy societal norms for decent housing by lowering the costs of renovation. To keep costs and rents low, City Homes emphasizes repair over replacement. It retains as much of the existing interior as possible and avoids unnecessary amenities.

The City Homes minimal-rehab approach does not require waivers from housing codes. It does require a willingness on the part of local and state officials to commit low-interest mortgage money to a project that is not a gut rehab. City Homes has renovated 243 row homes for an average of $12,000 each, and charges rent of $268 a month.

Because its costs are low, it can choose only tenants with a demonstrated ability to pay and willingness to maintain their households. The combined effect of reduced costs and good screening policies is the creation of a new, low-end rung on the housing ladder: nonrent-subsidized, low-income tenants who seek the chance to begin the process of upward mobility.

Creating homeownership opportunities. Homeownership is critical to the housing ladder system. Ownership gives lower-income families a stake in maintaining their property, increasing their investment, and moving up the ladder. Unfortunately, older, distressed urban neighborhoods sometimes offer little assurance that one's investment will be worthwhile.

Many builders recognize that another approach is possible: housing that is affordable not because it is subsidized but because it is cheap to build. The key to these opportunities for low-cost homeownership is open land, in the form of urban lots that are vacant or occupied by abandoned buildings. Two of the largest organizations engaged in such construction are nonprofits: the Nehemiah Plan Homes, in New York City, and Habitat for Humanity, the national organization headquartered in Americus, Georgia.

Nehemiah develops attached, single-family homes, owned by their residents, in once derelict areas. Nehemiah has, since 1984, built some 2,500 homes—mostly small row houses selling for between $51,000 to $73,000 on cleared land in Brooklyn and the Bronx. It is financed by two consortia of African-American churches, which provide no-interest financing by raising enough capital to get construction underway. Home sales replenish the capital and pay for the start of the next round of construction. In addition, Nehemiah homebuyers have received low-interest loans from a state agency.

Habitat for Humanity, which uses donated materials and volunteer labor, has become the 14th-largest homebuilder in the United States. Between 1984 and 1995, Habitat's 1,100 local chapters built some 40,000 modest single-family homes. The homes sell for as little as $30,000. Like Nehemiah, Habitat is self-financed, relying on donations for its capital. Unlike Nehemiah, it provides its own mortgage financing at no interest and redirects mortgage payments toward new construction. The homes it sells for $30,000 are typically valued at $50,000 or more. Often they are built on land given by government and improved through community-development grants.

Both Habitat and Nehemiah sell homes at below-market cost. They are, in other words, responding to that central complication of the housing ladder: the social consensus that we should not let the for-profit market alone provide housing at the bottom rungs. By deciding not to use price alone as a way to discriminate among buyers, Habitat and Nehemiah use other means that assure them of the reliability of their owner-occupants. Nehemiah looks for proof of ability to make payments, while Habitat uses both economic criteria and a questionnaire about personal character. Both groups limit the right to resell to discourage quick speculation.

Accessory apartments in Long Island. I have not advocated bringing subsidized rental programs to suburban locations. Such projects are likely to create a political backlash and to send the wrong message to less affluent families. Nevertheless, suburban municipalities need to recognize that neighborhoods change as the demand for housing types changes. Municipalities that adjust can continue to attract new residents and ensure stable or rising home values.

One model is laws that allow the creation of an accessory apartment in single-family homes, in effect converting them to two-family structures. Accessory units create a slightly lower, more accessible rung on the housing ladder for young, upwardly mobile residents. In the 1970s and 1980s, for example, many older, middle-class homeowners in the Long Island suburbs of New York found themselves paying high property taxes for homes with more space than they needed. So they began to rent out illegal accessory apartments, often converting basements or garages into separate living quarters. By changing their zoning laws, seven towns on Long Island, New York, helped to create thousands of new, legal housing units in the past 15 years.

It can be argued, of course, that the advent of accessory apartments is nothing less than a sign of deterioration. The fact is, however, that neighborhoods don't have as much choice as they think as to which rung they will occupy on the housing ladder. Acknowledging and adapting to incipient changes seems like a far better strategy than prohibition.

Some sort of subsidies are involved in some of the examples cited here. Such subsidies are limited and not necessary for the long-term financial management of the projects. Moreover, they are offset by the value of these examples' other attributes: low-cost construction, homeownership, and zoning and building code changes that enlarge our housing supply.

A Housing Policy That Recognizes the Housing Ladder

The transition to a housing policy that recognizes and rebuilds the housing ladder will be neither easy nor instant. The existing system of public and subsidized housing has powerful backing from various interest groups and bureaucracies. Finding humane ways to phase out these programs and incorporate public housing into the housing ladder will be difficult.

In addition to the practical and political obstacles to restoring the housing ladder, our society must also make a psychological transition. Somehow we must learn to accept the existence of poor, at times shabby, neighborhoods. Housing reformers discount the possibility that such neighborhoods can still serve their residents well, and that those residents might accept the challenge to improve their neighborhood or to improve their own prospects for moving elsewhere. Again and again, in American cities, the impulse to bulldoze poorer neighborhoods—lower rungs on the ladder—asserts itself. But there is no way that all neighborhoods can be middle class or better. And there is no sustainable way to replace inexpensive housing with a publicly subsidized alternative.

I do not propose specific new programs. The housing market is intensely local; officials must respect the market and make sure that regulations do not unnecessarily impede it. Rather, I offer a vision of incremental improvement, through individual initiative, altruism, and deregulation. The time has come for an approach that respects the way in which the private market improves the social character of neighborhoods. The restoration of the housing ladder will help not only the poor, but all of civil society.

> *"[Housing vouchers] give low-income families the opportunity to move to areas with lower crime, better schools, and cleaner neighborhoods."*

Housing Vouchers Benefit Low-Income Families

Merrill Matthews Jr.

Federal housing assistance generally falls into two categories: housing constructed and maintained at government expense, and Section 8 housing vouchers, which provide rental assistance to low-income families. In the following viewpoint, Merrill Matthews Jr. argues that the government should abandon public housing projects and instead fund more Section 8 vouchers. Unlike public housing projects, he contends, housing vouchers allow tenants the freedom to choose where they live. Furthermore, under the housing voucher program, tenants do not have to move when they are no longer eligible for federal subsidies. The author is the vice president for domestic policy at the National Center for Policy Analysis, a nonpartisan, nonprofit research institute based in Dallas, Texas.

As you read, consider the following questions:
1. What is the legacy of public housing, from the author's perspective?
2. According to Matthews, why do public housing authorities insist on building new structures?
3. As stated by the author, for the same amount of money the Dallas Housing Authority spent building homes for 75 families, what could it have provided in housing vouchers?

Excerpted from "Vouchers Come Home," by Merrill Matthews Jr., *Policy Review*, November/December 1998. Reprinted by permission of the Heritage Foundation.

Policymakers are finally beginning to recognize that introducing choice to public education will improve schooling. And new, bipartisan legislation in Congress suggests they have learned vouchers aren't just for education: Low-income families are demanding choice in public housing as well. As with educational choice, however, the government has not given up its outmoded thinking—like failed public-housing projects.

Today, more than a million families nationwide live in housing constructed and maintained at government expense. The legacy of this program is the countless high-rise apartment buildings that have become monuments to crime, drugs, joblessness, and hopelessness. As if the struggle facing low-income single mothers isn't hard enough, government policies have trapped many of them in war zones filled with despair.

These public housing projects are among the last crumbling edifices of central planning. Public housing in the United States was born in 1937 when Congress passed the Housing and Community Development Act. The original program offered loan guarantees to subsidize the construction of affordable housing for low-income working families. But it also created housing authorities to run and manage public housing, thus creating a strong constituency for building more and more housing projects.

Fortunately, the federal government offers an alternative: housing vouchers that supplement the rent low-income families pay and permit them to live where they choose. In 1974, Congress passed the Housing and Community Development Act, commonly known as the Section 8 housing assistance program. This program provides rental assistance primarily to families with incomes at or below 50 percent of the area's median income. Families who receive vouchers must pay up to a third of their income in rent; the average is about $163 per month. This "tenant-based" voucher is one of the most popular programs because it allows families to move wherever they choose. Yet, even as Congress moves to expand choice in housing assistance, somehow the government can't seem to shake its faith in publicly owned projects.

Public Housing Still Being Built

In 1996, under then-Secretary Henry Cisneros, the U.S. Department of Housing and Urban Development (HUD) took a step in the right direction by deciding to demolish about 100,000 "severely distressed" public housing units by the year 2003. Although 69,000 units have since been approved for demolition, only 25,000 to 30,000 have actually been torn down. Nevertheless, in most cities where old public-housing projects are coming down, new public housing is going up, albeit in much smaller numbers than before. HUD's goal is to replace about 40,000 of the 100,000 demolished units with new housing and to provide the other 60,000 families with Section 8 housing vouchers. . . .

Why do public housing authorities insist on building new structures, even as they tear down the old ones? For one thing, they provide construction jobs and money for local businesses, which—to put it delicately—may have supported various public officials. Another reason is that new bureaucrats always think they are smarter than old bureaucrats. Officials today say it was a mistake to concentrate all those low-income families in low-income areas, and it was a mistake to build high-rises that don't match the surrounding architecture. But if we build today's public housing differently, they say, we won't repeat yesterday's problems.

Current wisdom says that building a smaller number of single-family units that blend with the local architecture—usually clusters of townhouses—will solve all the old problems. Today's public-housing advocates need to be reminded that many of the housing projects built in the 1940s and 1950s were designed as high-rises because many architects considered tall buildings the wave of the future. Single-family townhouses aren't a refinement of public-housing design; they merely express the architectural bias of our time. (The only advantage of townhouses is that when the next generation of housing officials recognize their mistake, townhouses will be much easier and cheaper to demolish.)

Another way public-housing authorities hope to avoid the failures of the past is by placing some of the public housing units in higher-income areas, so they have access to safer neighborhoods, better schools, and well-paying jobs. The idea is to help at least a limited number of welfare recipients break the cycle of poverty by moving them out of poverty-stricken areas.

Of course, building low-income housing units in high-income areas also prompts political opposition from home-owners concerned about depressing property values. But the real problem with this approach is that it ignores the needs and preferences of low-income families. For example, those who depend on other family members often prefer to live close to them. Placing low-income parents in high-income areas often separates them from supportive extended families. If mom can't pick up a child after school, grandma may have to drive miles across town.

The Expensive Mistake of Public Housing

But these practical concerns are only one part of the public policy problem; the other is financial. It costs a lot more to build a house than it does to help a poor person rent one. Consider the ongoing public-housing controversy in Dallas. In 1995, U.S. District Judge Jerry Buchmeyer ruled in a lawsuit by a group of poor black women that government-sanctioned policies had forced thousands of low-income black families to live in slums. He ordered the Dallas Housing Authority (DHA) to provide Section 8 housing vouchers so that most of these families could live where they wanted. However, he also ordered the DHA to build 474 public housing apartments in predominantly white and higher-income areas, a task the DHA was eager to fulfill.

In addition, the DHA decided to demolish all 3,500 housing units that were the object of the lawsuit, even though it had already spent $20 million renovating them, and build about 950 units in their place. The first 225 of these have recently been completed. The total cost for the new housing, which is still located in low-income, high-crime areas, is expected to reach $57 million, or $60,000 per unit, excluding maintenance and the $20 million in wasted renovations.

But that's a bargain compared to the money Dallas has spent to build housing in higher-income areas. In May 1998, the DHA opened the first of the court-ordered public-housing projects to be built in higher-income areas of Dallas and its suburbs, and selected families began to move into the 75-unit townhouse complex. The complex alone cost about $4.9 million to build, and to purchase the land the DHA spent $1.3 million, more than $300,000 above its appraised value. Thus the city spent more than $82,000 per housing unit, excluding ongoing security and maintenance costs.

Vouchers Will Help Families Move Closer to Jobs

In today's booming economy, about two-thirds of new jobs are being created in the suburbs—far from where many low-income families live. The new housing vouchers that are part of the President's new budget will help families move closer to a new job, reduce a long commute, or secure more stable housing that will help them get or keep a job.

White House Office of the Press Secretary, December 29, 1999.

Of course, the new townhouses will last a while, so might the expenditure pay off in the long run? The answer is no. One of the main problems with building public housing is that people are encouraged to stay on the public dole. They often—though not always—get nicer, newer homes from the government than they could otherwise afford even with Section 8 vouchers. That acts as a disincentive to find work, because a family that earned enough to lose its public assistance would have to move. Those with housing vouchers, by contrast, could stay where they are; they would just pay full rent.

Welfare reform has been successful at both the state and federal levels because it aspires to move every recipient off welfare within a few years. In other words, cash assistance is temporary. Unfortunately, this policy of time limits has not been extended as aggressively to public housing. With vouchers, however, subsidies could be gradually reduced with rising income, easing the transition off assistance without forcing families to move.

"Tenant Choice"

The desire to bring the benefits of higher-income neighborhoods to low-income families could be extended to more people if the government would tame its urge to build more public housing. For the same amount of money the Dallas Housing Authority spent on building homes for 75 families, it could have provided 200 families with $5,000 a year in housing vouchers for six years. And those families could have lived where they chose rather than where a federal judge said they had to live. Call it "tenant choice."

According to an analysis done by the *Dallas Morning News*, by the end of March 1998, more than 1,800 low-income families—80 percent of them black—were using Section 8 housing vouchers to live in largely middle-class, white areas of Dallas and its suburbs. Thus, while 75 families are pinned down to one location, 1,800 have the freedom to go wherever jobs, family, or good schools draw them. Fourteen of these low-income families live within blocks of a new 40-unit, court-ordered public-housing project still under construction—at a fraction of the cost of the new townhouses.

The benefits of vouchers to these families are many. They give low-income families the opportunity to move to areas with lower crime, better schools, and cleaner neighbor-hoods. In addition, vouchers are more compatible with the idea that public-housing assistance, like any type of welfare, should be temporary.

Reforming the welfare system by putting welfare recipi-ents to work and announcing lifetime limits on aid has been a phenomenal success. Nationwide, welfare rolls have de-clined 42 percent since their peak in 1994, and several states have experienced a drop of 60 percent or more. Yet public housing, which is another way states and the federal govern-ment supplement poor families' income, has yet to be ad-dressed sufficiently by welfare reform. Like open-ended en-titlements, building public housing implies—and may even encourage—long-term public assistance.

*"With the rental market sizzling, . . .
landlords have discovered they can easily
find unsubsidized clients willing to pay
escalating rents and no longer need . . .
poorer tenants paying below-market rates."*

Housing Vouchers Do Not Always Benefit Low-Income Families

Ann O'Hanlon

A federal program that provides housing vouchers for low-income tenants—known as Section 8—has helped millions of families to find safe, affordable housing. However, contends Ann O'Hanlon in the following viewpoint, landlords are increasingly refusing to accept Section 8 vouchers; in the Washington, D.C., area, approximately half of the landlords who used to accept vouchers no longer do so. According to O'Hanlon, landlords can make more profit and avoid bureaucratic regulations by rejecting tenants with vouchers. O'Hanlon is a *Washington Post* staff writer.

As you read, consider the following questions:

1. What are the signs of the voucher crisis across the country, as stated by O'Hanlon?
2. According to the author, what is the trade-off for higher subsidized rents?
3. What must a property owner do to become a Section 8 landlord, as described by the author?

Reprinted from "Boom Times a Bust for Housing Subsidy: Area Landlords Won't Take Vouchers," by Ann O'Hanlon, *The Washington Post*, July 25, 2000, with permission. Copyright © 2000, The Washington Post.

S he loved her old apartment: outdoor fountains at the building's entrance, a view from a spacious sixth-floor balcony, a laundry room on every floor. A child of Detroit's ghetto, Cynthia Evans thought living at London Park Towers in Alexandria, Virginia, "was one of the few times in my life where I felt like a normal person."

Then her landlord broke the news. London Park was raising rents and, more important, no longer would accept the federal voucher that had allowed her to live there for six years. Evans either had to pay the higher rent without the federal help—an impossibility—or move out in 60 days. Her once-crippling depression returned; she again felt suicidal. "When I got that notice, it just—I almost OD'd," she said.

Now a cockroach-laden building with poor security is her home.

Hundreds of the working poor locally—and thousands across the country—are being squeezed out of their apartments into less desirable ones or onto waiting lists as many private landlords opt out of a huge federal rent subsidy program.

With the rental market sizzling, the landlords have discovered they can easily find unsubsidized clients willing to pay escalating rents and no longer need to fill out their buildings by accepting poorer tenants paying below-market rates through the program, called Section 8.

The owner of a Prince George's County apartment complex, for example, just told 300 tenants who use Section 8 that they had to be out by the end of September.

"A Business Decision"

"It's definitely a business decision," said Dave Thomas, director of property management for Allen and Rocks, which oversees the Washington Heights Apartments. The owner, Nalbel Limited Partnership, believes it can "get better rents and not have to deal with the bureaucracy of the federal government."

As a result of the Section 8 crunch, officials say, homeless rolls are rising—up 12 percent in Fairfax County, for example—and qualified Section 8 families are waiting longer for a slot in a shrunken universe of landlords still willing to participate in the program.

All this comes at a time when other options for the poor,

such as public housing, are diminishing as well. Pam Michell, who runs New Hope Housing in Fairfax County, a private group, said the Section 8 situation has never been worse in her 16-year career.

"It used to be if someone got a Section 8, we could sort of breathe a sigh of relief and say, 'Oh, these folks are going to be okay,' "Michell said. "Now I see them get one and I think, 'Oh God, they got a Section 8.'"

Under the program, which is administered through local housing officials, the low-income participants pay a portion of an apartment's rent and the federal government covers the rest, up to a fixed maximum. But in many cases, that maximum is now below the rent the apartment could command in the open market. According to Delta Associates, the vacancy rate in the region is less than 1 percent. Rents have increased 15 percent in some cases since last year.

Translation: Section 8 renters are no longer enticing to many landlords, especially given the program's paperwork requirements. They can make more profit without it.

"I guess a lot of the landlords that may have needed us before don't need us anymore," said Peggy Pimenthal, Arlington County's housing director.

No one knows how many Section 8-related units in the region have evaporated—there used to be 32,000—in part because of how the program works.

In some cases, landlords agree to designate all or some of the units in a building as available for Section 8 tenants, and housing officials then direct them to those buildings. So when a participating landlord takes a building off the list, the units lost are readily known to officials. To date, landlords of such designated buildings have withdrawn about 1,000 apartments from the pool.

Saying No to Vouchers

In other cases, tenants are not directed to buildings available to Section 8 applicants but are given a voucher, good for a limited period, that they can give to any landlord willing to take it as partial payment of the rent. Because this type of Section 8 is decentralized, it is difficult to quantify how many landlords who used to say yes to vouchers are now saying no.

But a survey of 200 local landlords and housing offices by the *Washington Post* suggests that about half the landlords in Fairfax and Prince George's counties who used to accept vouchers no longer do. Twelve of the 31 landlords in Alexandria who did have stopped doing so. Many prospective tenants describe fruitlessly calling 100 or more landlords.

Rob Rogers. Reprinted by permission of United Feature Syndicate, Inc.

Ernette Starks, 33, who lives with her three children at the Washington Heights complex in Prince George's, is scrambling to find a new place before the September 30 deadline. But, she said, landlords have told her either that they won't take a Section 8 voucher or that the waiting list for the few units they devote to the program is long. So long, Starks said, that "you'll be on the street before they have a place for you." And if a voucher expires before being used, its holder must return to the waiting list and start over.

Kay Management, which operates Cynthia Evans's former building, decided it would no longer participate in Section 8 there and at two other Alexandria locations because of government paperwork and because the subsidies left rents too far below market rates, a spokeswoman said.

Banners at London Park Towers now tout "our new look"

and "fantastic designer kitchens," and the rent on Evans's former unit is now $865, up from $810. The building's rents will soon climb even higher, said Suzanne Higgs, Kay Management's regional property manager.

"We're moving it from a Class B property to a Class A property," Higgs said, adding that the effect on Section 8 residents was sad. "When they say, 'This is my home,' we feel it, because we're human, too, but we have a responsibility to the owners, too."

In her search for new accommodations, Evans, 30, had two options. One was the homeless shelter where she works as a mental health counselor, giving seminars on how to survive mental illness. The other was the bug-infested building she ultimately chose. She didn't think living among clients at the shelter would send the right message.

"It's kind of hard to set yourself up as a person who's coping when you've just been evicted," Evans said, only half-joking.

Signs of the Crisis

Signs of the crisis abound across the country. Homeless shelters in Boston have overflowed for 24 consecutive months, a record. In San Francisco, the federal Department of Housing and Urban Development (HUD) raised its subsidy ceiling by 50 percent, trying to keep pace with high rents. In a trial program, Seattle's Housing Authority allowed Section 8 recipients to use as much income for rent as they felt they could afford—rather than holding them to 30 percent—in the hope they could hang on to units. Many tenants in the trial program found they had to pay half their income, even with Uncle Sam's help, to have their own roof.

To complaints that they are not adapting to the rising rental market, HUD officials reply that new laws are in place to help and that local governments need to be creative and aggressive in marketing the program.

"HUD does not entirely control conditions and circumstances within the local market," said Gloria Cousar, a deputy assistant secretary. "Local communities themselves can offer incentives such as tax deductions or tax credits."

Indeed, some jurisdictions are finding piecemeal solutions. Montgomery County, for example, has not lost many Section 8 units because it helps nonprofit organizations buy complexes that landlords are threatening to take out of the program. The Housing Initiative Fund was just approved for another year, to the tune of $7 million.

Beyond that, some local governments are issuing even more Section 8 vouchers, to guarantee that in a diminished market, all the landlords still willing to accept one are found by apartment seekers, much the way airlines overbook flights to make sure every seat is filled.

And Arlington, Fairfax and Montgomery counties, as well as Alexandria, just raised by 10 percent the maximum rent they are willing to help cover, a new option made possible by HUD and Congress. That means, for example, that government will help underwrite a $924 apartment instead of an $840 one, presumably making it more attractive for landlords to participate. The District is on the verge of taking a similar step.

(There's a trade-off for the higher subsidized rents. Jurisdictions get a finite pot of Section 8 money from Uncle Sam. Bigger subsidies mean the money does not underwrite as many apartments overall.)

Little Cause to Accept Vouchers

Even with adjustments, many landlords have little cause other than a good heart to open their doors to government assistance. Jan Landskroner, a senior citizen in Alexandria, was fortunate to have that happen.

Landskroner, a former teacher who is now disabled, got word a year ago that her home of eight years, the Foxchase apartments, might abandon the Section 8 program, possibly forcing 423 tenants to look elsewhere. Then the landlord agreed to a five-year renewal of its Section 8 participation after government agreed to do better with subsidies.

Even so, Landskroner said, "It's inhuman, particularly for the disabled and elderly people, to be put through this." And even with the agreement, the landlord is falling behind again. Two-bedroom apartments could go for $1,410 a month on the open market now, but under the agreement, the subsidies will reach only to $1,150.

"I think we could have probably made more money in

the long run by opting out," said Bruce Terwilliger, senior vice president with Aimco, the Foxchase landlord. "But we want to be good citizens. . . . We want to be supportive of the community."

Landlords Don't Like the Hassle

Many landlords, however, just don't like the hassle.

To become a Section 8 landlord, a property owner must fill out three or four forms and then wait for a government inspection. The lease must contain some government language, which many landlords say is more restrictive than their typical lease. Once the Section 8 tenant is in place, a form or two must be signed each year, and the local housing authority, as well as the tenant, must be notified of any rent increase or eviction.

It sounds like a lot, said Kim Berry, the property manager for a Fairfax homeless-prevention program and Section 8 landlord called Good Shepherd Housing. But, she said, in reality, the paperwork "takes maybe 15 minutes a year."

Paperwork aside, other landlords complain that government checks sometimes arrive late. And some acknowledge that they would rather not have Section 8 tenants at all because apartments sometimes wind up damaged.

Marjorie Kennedy Pantaleo, who runs a transitional housing program in Prince William County, said she understands landlords' reluctance. Just the same, she said, they could help fix the problem. "They could screen people better, get good references and really pay attention," Pantaleo said.

Amid all this turbulence and change sits Jelanda Winston, 22, holding a Section 8 voucher she'd love to use. Her mother died of cancer last year, leaving Winston, a child care worker, with four dependents in a two-bedroom apartment in Reston. Her two young brothers sleep on cushions on the living room floor, and her sister sleeps on a fold-out cushion at the foot of her daughter's bed. The belongings of four children are stuffed into one closet.

One brother, Ammiel, 12, pines for a room where he and his brother could display their L.A. Lakers posters. "I would like my own room to relax in and do my own stuff," he said. "I could do homework in my room."

But Winston can find no landlord willing to accept the

Section 8 voucher for a three-bedroom apartment. It will expire next month.

How Section 8 Works

The Housing and Community Development Act of 1974 created the affordable housing program known today as Section 8. Costing $14 billion in fiscal 2000, it serves 3 million households across the country by providing them rent subsidies.

People qualify if they are at or below a certain income level, which varies across the country according to a region's median income.

A typical eligible family of four in the Washington area has an income of about $24,000, but even eligible families often have to wait years before receiving the voucher to take to landlords. Montgomery County just opened its waiting list for the first time since 1992, and Fairfax County estimates that anyone on its list will wait five years.

When a family finally receives a voucher, it is good for a set amount of rent—$1,145 for a three-bedroom apartment, for example. The family must pay 30 percent of its income toward the rent, and the government makes up the difference.

> "Besides offering decent housing to the homeless, hapless or mentally ill, supported SROs have saved some old buildings ... from dereliction."

SROs Offer a Solution to Homelessness

The Economist

Many commentators argue that the diminishing supply of single-room-occupancy (SRO) units—modest one-room apartments with low rents—has led to an increase in homelessness. In the following viewpoint, *The Economist*, a weekly political magazine, maintains that new SRO developments offer a safe, inexpensive housing option for the homeless. A New York City SRO development, which allocates half of the units to the extremely poor and half to low-income working families, has proven a success.

As you read, consider the following questions:

1. How is the city of New York helping nonprofit agencies create new SROs, as stated by the author?
2. What evidence does the author provide that SROs are cheaper than the alternatives?
3. According to *The Economist*, what are the benefits of mixed-income housing?

Reprinted from "Room at the Top: Housing for the Poor," editorial, *The Economist*, June 1, 1996, by permission of the New York Times Special Features. Copyright © 1996, The Economist, Ltd.

If it seems at first glance that the hall of Grand Central Station and the grates of New York have fewer vagrants than they did a few years ago, the impression is correct. The population of the city's shelters has fallen from a high of 12,000 a night in the late 1980s to about 7,000 now. Many of the formerly homeless people have gone into new single-room apartments.

The growth of such apartments, which are designed for single people only, is a reversal of previous policy. In 1960 the city had 142,000 single-room-occupancy (SRO) units. By 1985, thanks to its decision to redevelop many of these and not to approve replacements, only 42,000 were left. Meanwhile, New York state has since 1974 released some 200,000 psychiatric patients into "community care". The number of homeless people has soared.

Now the city is helping non-profit agencies to create new SROs once more. City-provided loans for the units have reached a total of $261m. The state has chipped in a subsidy to pay for support services, such as TB testing and employment assistance. The city now has 10,500 beds in "supported SROs", and around 35,000 private rooms. Besides offering decent housing to the homeless, hapless or mentally ill, supported SROs have saved some old buildings, such as the Times Square Hotel in midtown Manhattan, from dereliction.

Cheaper than the Alternatives

In the long run, surprisingly, providing a private room, with a kitchenette and bath, is cheaper than the alternatives. A 15-square-metre room in a supported SRO costs New York city $12,500 a year to run, compared with $20,000 for a space in a public shelter and $113,000 for a psychiatric bed in hospital. The main reason for this saving is that supported SROs can ensure that residents claim all their benefits, such as disabled veterans' allowances or pensions forgone, and then take a portion of them as rent. Shelters, by contrast, house a drifting population in nobody's care who cannot easily be charged anything.

Some of the larger SROs set aside space for local residents. This blunts neighbourhood opposition, and also avoids clumping too many needy, homeless or mentally ill people together. At Times Square, for example, half the 652 units are reserved for working people on less than $25,000 a year. They pay a top rent of $495 a month. By mixing its tenants, the building—New York's largest supported SRO—keeps on an even keel. "Everyone thought this would be a noble failure," says Rosanne Haggerty, president of Common Ground Community, which founded and runs the place. Now New York boasts about it.

A Sense of Community

Despite the small rooms, [SRO] residents seem happy. The studios are bright and secure. Mario Capuano, who was formerly homeless, says the residence provides him with people to support him and talk to him—a sense of community. He uses the kitchen to cook his own meals. "Basically, I'm independent," says Mr. Capuano.

Ron Scherer, *Christian Science Monitor*, March 7, 1997.

The Times Square building has been full since opening day, and is averaging less than one eviction a month; it has a 14-month waiting list for new tenants. Residents work in the downstairs ice-cream shop and also help to maintain the building. Even the neighbours like it; the cleaned-up building has improved the look of the street and the tenants have not misbehaved. Common Ground plans to repeat the idea at another nearby abandoned welfare hotel.

An Experiment in Mixed-Income Housing

Another experiment in mixed-income housing is the Neighbour Entrepreneurs Programme, which began last year. The city is subsidizing private property managers to renovate and buy 200 city-owned apartment buildings. Roughly three-quarters of the units will be reserved, for 20 years, for lower-income occupants, but the landlords can rent the rest at market rates. Eventually, the hope is to have 10,000 units in the scheme. If it works, the city will have an improved stock of low-income housing, landlords will make money, and the buildings will have a better mix of tenants.

Yet it will be an uphill struggle. New York state's $4 billion deficit is cramping all spending. Federal programmes for low-income housing may be killed. And making SROs profitable for private builders is a task that would humble Hercules. A city advisory board concluded that it would require 35 pages of changes in the regulatory code, just for a start.

"[SROs] are both expensive ... and inadequate."

SROs Are Currently an Inadequate Solution to Homelessness

British Columbia Ministry of Social Development and Economic Security

Single room occupancy (SRO) units, one-room apartments that often house the extremely poor, are neither inexpensive nor safe, holds the British Columbia's Ministry of Social Development and Economic Security in the following viewpoint. In the author's view, these units cost more per square foot than most rental housing and are usually plagued by squalid conditions. SROs may provide a last resource for the homeless, claims the author, but they are not a solution to homelessness. The Ministry of Social Development and Economic Security is a department of the government of Canada's province of British Columbia. The ministry's goal is to create a society in which all people have access to quality, affordable, sustainable housing and child care, jobs, and, where necessary, income support.

As you read, consider the following questions:

1. What are the three main reasons that SROs are usually occupied by lower income singles, as claimed by the author?
2. How does the author describe the conditions of most SROs?
3. What threatens SRO hotels, in the author's view?

Excerpted from *Nowhere to Live: A Call to Action by the Lower Income Urban Singles Task Group*, published by the British Columbia Ministry of Social Development and Economic Security at www.sdes.gov.bc.ca/housing/NOWHERE?part1b.html. Reprinted with permission.

There are an estimated 13,000 to 15,000 hotel and motel rooms in B.C. that are used primarily for residential purposes. These SRO (Single Room Occupancy) units, as they're known, are located in the central core of virtually every city in the province. They are both expensive (on a per-foot basis) and inadequate, usually equipped with neither washroom nor cooking facilities.

SROs are usually occupied by lower income singles—people on income assistance or working for low wages—for three main reasons:

1. Because of their limited size, SRO units can usually only accommodate single occupants.
2. SRO hotels are often located in areas that have other services and networks for people with low incomes.
3. They are the only housing resource that a single person with a limited income can afford without a subsidy.

Increasingly the people who live in SROs are those with special needs—for example, people with physical disabilities, chronic mental illness, chronic drug and alcohol abuse, or HIV/AIDS.

Apalling Conditions

Conditions in SROs are often appalling. Buildings are usually old and squalid. Cockroaches and rodents are rampant. Communal washroom facilities are over-used and frequently filthy. Tenant safety and security measures may be non-existent, resulting in an environment that is at best threatening, and often dangerous. Rooms may be cold in winter, unbearably hot in the summer. The lack of cooking facilities and refrigerators in many SROs makes it more difficult and more expensive for tenants to have a nutritious diet, and often has a major impact on their health. (Most rely on soup kitchens and food banks.) And residents of some better-maintained motels may be forced to move out during tourist season, as rents are increased sharply to daily rates and the rooms used for tourist accommodation.

Ironically, SROs actually cost more than most rental housing. The average SRO is about 100 square feet of living space and rents for $325 per month—or $3.25 per square foot. In Vancouver, the average rent for a one-bedroom apartment is $645, or about $1 per square foot. What makes SROs appear to be affordable rental housing is their lower than average total monthly rent—not what you get for the money. And in most cases, the rent for an SRO is much greater than 30 per cent of a tenant's monthly income.

A Long, Slow Decline

Residential hotels haven't always been the bottom of the rental market. The hotel as a form of housing emerged in the 18th century and peaked late in the 19th century. In North American cities, hotels were used by urban people of all class backgrounds, from wealthy professionals to migratory workers and homeless men, and represented the freedom and mobility of urban living, especially for women, who were released from cooking and other household work.

After the Depression and the Second World War, however, when society had begun to idealize the nuclear family and suburban home ownership, hotel and apartment living were no longer viewed as respectable. Unmarried people and transients were seen as social outsiders. By the 1950s, the hotel was considered to be the most undesirable form of housing, and its tenants were seen to be irresponsible, untrustworthy and undeserving of rights or assistance.

"Like Living in a Prison"

Ken Roberts, a 48-year-old native of Guyana, spent eight hellish months in 1995 in a commercial SRO. . . . "Living in an SRO was like living in a prison," said Roberts. "No cooking was allowed, and we only had a bed and basic bathroom facilities. They treated us like the dregs of society." He said staff became violent when the residents complained about unsanitary conditions. During Roberts' stay in the hotel, two men killed each other in a drug-related shooting.

Dylan Foley, *Body Positive*, September 1998.

The new high-rise hotels of the 1960s, accommodating exclusively tourists and traveling professionals, were the last nail in the coffin for SRO hotels. Home now mainly to the cities' poorest residents, most could no longer be run for a profit, and went without maintenance, becoming increasingly dilapidated. By the 1970s, thousands of SRO units had been lost to condemnation and fire, as well as to the process of urban renewal and development. With little low rent housing to replace these units, the number of people who were homeless increased dramatically.

In the months before Expo '86 in Vancouver, private owners of SRO hotels, planning to cash in on thousands of anticipated tourists, upgraded their rooms and evicted hundreds of long-term tenants. It was only through the media attention given to these events that the public finally began to recognize the importance of SROs as a kind of safety net reducing absolute homelessness.

As defined by the United Nations: Absolute homelessness or shelterlessness refers to individuals living in the streets with no physical shelter.

Relative homelessness refers to people living in spaces that do not meet basic health and safety standards, including:
- protection from the elements
- access to safe water and sanitation
- security of tenure and personal safety
- affordability.

Even This Is Threatened

Yet even with the recognition of the important role of SRO hotels as a last resource for people who would otherwise be without shelter, the number of SRO units has continued to decline. In Vancouver alone, for example, over 900 SRO units (11 per cent) have been lost in the last nine years, or about 100 per year. SRO units have also been lost in most other urban centres in B.C. This decline has obviously contributed to the increased numbers of homeless people in our communities.

SRO hotels are threatened by:
- age and neglect, often leading to building closures
- fire
- conversion to tourist accommodation
- demolition and redevelopment.

In most cases, because of their desirable urban locations, SROs are replaced with commercial buildings rather than housing.

SRO hotels are neither adequate nor affordable housing: by United Nations definitions, people who live in SROs in B.C. are relatively homeless. And yet they are essential, in that they keep people from becoming absolutely shelterless. They are a standard housing resource for low income singles, and increasingly for those with special needs.

Clearly, SROs must be preserved. While they are not the answer to homelessness, and should never be seen as a permanent solution, SROs can be a key component to an overall strategy to end homelessness. As SROs continue to be lost, homelessness will inevitably continue to increase.

Periodical Bibliography

The following articles have been selected to supplement the diverse views presented in this chapter. Addresses are provided for periodicals not indexed in the *Readers' Guide to Periodical Literature*, the *Alternative Press Index*, the *Social Sciences Index*, or the *Index to Legal Periodicals and Books*.

Nina Bernstein
"Rent Subsidies Proposed for Homeless Families," *The New York Times*, October 12, 2000.

Business Wire
"New Information Shows Supportive Housing Effective, Economical Solution to Homelessness," May 17, 2000.

Marlene Cimons
"Clinton Doling Out $1 Billion for Homeless," *Los Angeles Times*, December 16, 1999.

Evan Halper and Stephanie McCrummen
"Out of Sight, Out of Mind: New York City's New Homeless Policy," *Washington Monthly*, April 1998.

Robert V. Hess
"Helping People Off the Streets, Real Solutions to Urban Homelessness," *USA Today*, January 18–20, 2000.

Kim Hopper
"Housing the Homeless," *Social Policy*, Spring 1998.

Howard Husock
"Let's End Housing Vouchers: The Politically Popular Section 8 Program Ruins Neighborhoods and Perpetuates Poverty," *City Journal*, Autumn 2000. Available from the Manhattan Institute, 52 Vanderbilt Ave., 2nd Floor, New York, NY 10017.

Christopher Jencks
"Half-Right on Public Housing," *The New York Times*, May 20, 1997.

Guy Lawson
"Down and Out at the Hotel Providence," *Harper's*, December 1999.

Ron Scherer
"Comfort and Style for the Homeless," *Christian Science Monitor*, March 7, 1997.

Julie Tamaki
"Habitat for Humanity Helps Families Build Better Future," *Los Angeles Times*, December 6, 1998.

Bonnie L. Voss and Gary L. Harke
"Empower: Beyond Homelessness to Affordable Housing," *Christian Social Action*, July/August, 1998. Available from University Microfilm, Ann Arbor, MI 48106.

Washington Post
"Clueless on the Homeless," May 14, 2000.

CHAPTER 4

How Should Society Deal with the Homeless?

Chapter Preface

On February 8, 2000, William Anthony Miller, a homeless man who suffered from mental illness, was shot to death for lunging at police with a tree branch. In the view of some commentators, this incident and others like it demonstrate that laws need to be strengthened to allow the seriously mentally ill to be committed to hospital care.

Before the 1960s, most of the seriously mentally ill resided in state hospitals. However, after it was discovered that many mental illnesses could be treated with medication, policymakers reasoned that patients would be better served through outpatient care. The process of deinstitutionalization, which occurred during the 1960s and 1970s, led to the release of over eight hundred thousand mentally ill patients from institutions. Many of these released patients, too debilitated to seek care, became homeless.

Consequently, opponents of deinstitutionalization maintain that some of the homeless mentally ill who wander the nation's streets would be better off if they were committed—even against their will—to institutions or treatment programs. As psychiatrist E. Fuller Torrey explains, "Society has an obligation to help those who can not help themselves before their illness escalates to tragedy. . . . [M]andatory treatment for those too ill to understand their need for treatment is a much more humane intervention than what we have now: mandatory non-treatment."

Not everyone agrees, however, that a return to stricter commitment laws is a good idea. John Ho and Carol Patterson of the National Empowerment Center on the West Coast contend that the basis of such laws is the belief that people with untreated mental illnesses pose a threat to society—a belief they state is patently false. Moreover, they claim, a comprehensive study conducted by New York's Bellevue Hospital reveals that voluntary mental health services are as effective as involuntary commitment in treating the mentally ill.

In the following chapter, authors discuss in greater detail the problem of how to help the homeless mentally ill. This chapter provides a variety of perspectives on society's role in helping the homeless and preventing homelessness.

> *"It is time to impose the sort of tough-love approach to the hardcore homeless that seems to be producing positive results."*

The Hardcore Homeless Should Be Arrested

David Brooks

In recent years, Rudy Giuliani, the mayor of New York City, has proposed that homeless people who refuse offers of shelter should be arrested, and that able-bodied homeless people should be required to work in return for their shelter. In the following viewpoint, David Brooks, a senior editor of the *Weekly Standard*, a conservative magazine, argues in favor of these and other measures that force the homeless off city streets. He maintains that such an approach is necessary to protect society from dangerous, drug-addicted vagrants.

As you read, consider the following questions:
1. What evidence does Brooks provide that New York is generous toward the homeless?
2. According to the author, what is the problem with the "hardcore homeless"?
3. What is the "tough-love" approach to the homeless problem, as described by the author?

Paris Drake is quite a piece of work. His criminal career started when he was 14, and he has been arrested 22 times in the intervening 18 years. Drake, a New York native who has no fixed address, has served time for drug-dealing, assault, weapons possession, larceny, and burglary. His prison sentences have ranged from a day to four years, and each time he was released he picked up where he left off. Then, on November 16, 1999, he became enraged because he couldn't raise enough money to buy crack. So he picked up a six-pound paving stone and hurled it at the back of Nicole Barrett's head. Barrett is a young office worker who just happened to be walking by. She suffered terrible head injuries and almost died.

Still a Lot of Evil, Dangerous People

The attack reminded New Yorkers that for all the amazing progress that has been made in bringing order to the city, there are still a lot of evil, dangerous people around. Mayor Rudolph Giuliani responded with measures to assert some authority over the hardest of the hardcore homeless. He proposed that street vagrants who refuse offers of shelter and violate the law should be issued summonses or arrested. He also announced that able-bodied homeless people who could work in exchange for their benefits should be asked to do so.

All hell broke loose. Rev. Al Sharpton rounded up the usual suspects for street protests. Hillary Clinton went to the New York Theological Seminary and blasted Giuliani's policies. She said they violated the Christmas spirit, which celebrates "the birth of a homeless child." She implied that Giuliani was driven merely by polls and said, "Criminalizing the homeless with mass arrests for those whose only offense is that they have no home is wrong." Mrs. Clinton promised that if elected senator, she will instead work to triple the value of new housing vouchers. Judge Elliot Wilk, a long-time activist judge on homeless matters, temporarily halted the mayor's plans.

The whole episode serves as a depressing reminder of how tough it is to change a political culture. Giuliani has spent the past six years trying to restore public authority in

New York. His efforts have produced obvious and remarkable improvements. You would think that some of his enemies would have been moved to rethink their policy views. Instead, they have worked ever more aggressively to topple Giuliani and roll back his programs. The Al Sharptons of the world still equate orderly streets with racism. Hillary Clinton tries to breathe new life into the liberal orthodoxies of the mid-seventies, as if homelessness were a failure of capitalism to provide cheap housing and not a consequence of the bungled deinstitutionalization of the mentally ill. Some minds are permanently closed.

Let's be clear about the true state of play in New York. The city has some of the most generous social provisions for the homeless in the country. It devotes $850 million a year to homeless services. New York is the only city in the country that by law must offer shelter to every homeless person who requests it. No one is turned away.

The Hardcore Homeless Do Not Want Shelter

The problem is that many of the hardcore homeless do not want shelter. These are not just unfortunate individuals down on their luck. They are not families cast out of housing because of economic crisis. Disproportionately, they are mentally ill, often schizophrenic. Most have some serious addiction. Most lead horrific lives. They are beaten and robbed, and occasionally beat and rob in turn. Hillary Clinton may have some romanticized image of the homeless as Mary, Joseph, and baby Jesus, but this has nothing to do with the reality of homelessness as it is experienced by people who don't ride in motorcades.

The city of New York and private groups have undertaken noble and high-minded efforts to try to coax these people into shelters, where they can be given medication and treated. The Times Square Business Improvement District (BID) procured over $2.5 million in state and federal money to hire teams of social service professionals to roam the streets, trying to persuade vagrants to visit the new "respite center." Over the first year of the program, BID spent $700,000 and managed to persuade all of *two* people to accept housing. To its credit, BID hired a journalism professor to write up a candid report on the effort, which was in turn picked up by Heather Mac Donald in the *City Journal*. (If there were any justice in the world, Mac Donald would be knee-deep in Pulitzer Prizes and National Magazine Awards for her pioneering work on homelessness and other urban issues.)

Linking Shelter to Work

In 1979, New York became the first city in America to grant a guaranteed right to shelter. Mr. Giuliani wants to end this, by making shelter conditional on the homeless person working.

Linking shelter to work may not be as heartless as it seems. The city will provide a job, if a private alternative is not available. And it will provide childcare for homeless mothers while they work (though a suggestion that mothers refusing to work might have their children taken into care when they are put out on to the streets has generated some hostile publicity). The requirement to work would apply only to the "able-bodied"—probably less than 20% of those in single-person shelters, and slightly more in family shelters, says a city official.

The Economist, January 29, 2000.

The report describes the non-threatening approach adopted by the BID social workers. One day the workers came across a large cardboard box on the sidewalk across the street from the *New York Times* building, with a dirty hand sticking out. They noticed the hand was moving, so figuring the body attached to it must be okay, they moved on. They came across a man known as Shoeshine Bill with swollen ankles sitting in a puddle of his own urine. He assured them he was doing fine so they moved on. A young couple was lying on the street, the woman in the advanced stages of alcoholism. They declined to go to the shelter, though the man joked they'd be willing to go for an hour if they could get a private room with a bed. Another vagrant, known as Heavy, barricaded himself behind some mail carts when he saw the social workers coming.

Many of these people are not capable of thinking in their own long-term self-interest. In the short term, they see little need to go to places where they can get treatment, because activist groups bring food and clothing straight to their boxes—a delivery service that keeps the homeless untreated and fresh in the minds of the public.

Prodding the Homeless to Take Responsibility for Themselves

The Giuliani administration says it is time to impose the sort of tough-love approach to the hardcore homeless that seems to be producing positive results as part of welfare reform. That means prodding the homeless to take responsibility for themselves, whenever possible, by working for their benefits. It also means building on serious efforts, undertaken in dozens of cities nationwide, to get the homeless off the streets. Mrs. Clinton talks of mass arrests for the crime of lacking shelter, but that is sheer demagoguery. Since Giuliani ordered New York police to intensify their efforts to rein in homelessness, the cops have had contact with 1,674 homeless people. Of those, 380 were taken to a shelter, 67 were taken to a hospital for physical or mental treatment. Only 164 were arrested, often because there were prior warrants out for their arrest. The fact is, the Giuliani policy does distinguish between the many different sorts of people who are homeless. Compared with Mrs. Clinton's crude attacks, his policy is a model of nuanced sophistication.

Over the past 20 years, city after city, run by Democrats and Republicans, has tried to reassert public order. Mayors have argued that the liberty of the homeless doesn't necessarily trump the interests of the community. Nobody has a right to defecate in doorways, intimidate pedestrians, and menace store owners. In this new era, an attempt is being made to balance liberty and license with civility and order.

But as with most political struggles, there is never a conclusion. The liberationists sense they are gaining strength. They sense that the voters in New York now take the gains of the past decade for granted and are weary of Rudy Giuliani's aggressive style. They sense an opportunity to return to the old policy regime, and they may be right. If they are, there will be more Paris Drakes out on the streets, and more Nicole Barretts in the hospitals.

"*Most advocates agree that city governments can begin to address the homelessness problem only by turning away from the criminalization approach.*"

Society Should Not Criminalize the Homeless

Karl Lydersen

In the viewpoint that follows, Karl Lydersen condemns local governments' attempts to "clean up" the homeless by arresting them for infractions such as sleeping on the streets, urinating in public, and possessing open containers of alcohol. Lydersen, a reporter at the *Washington Post* Chicago Bureau and associate editor of the newspaper *Streetwise*, holds that such arrests violate the civil rights of the homeless and do nothing to curb the problem of homelessness. If society truly wants to help the homeless, Lydersen contends, it will provide them with emergency shelter, drug treatment, and job counseling programs.

As you read, consider the following questions:
1. According to the author, when the homeless access social service organizations, what is the result?
2. List three examples of local governments' attempts to criminalize the homeless, as stated by the author.
3. Why is the homeless population increasing, according to Lydersen?

Reprinted, with permission, from "Out of Sight: In Many Cities, Being Homeless Is Against the Law," by Karl Lydersen, *In These Times*, June 12, 2000.

When the Department of Housing and Urban Development (HUD) released an intensive, three-year study on homelessness in December 1999, it proved what the homeless themselves have long known: Homelessness will continue to plague this country as long as cities fail to provide adequate shelter and social services.

The study, which involved the efforts of 12 federal agencies and thousands of interviews, showed that approximately 2 million people are homeless at some point during any given year, a third of whom had slept on the street or in some other public place within the last week. Families are the fastest-growing segment of the homeless population, and more working people are becoming homeless because of rising housing costs and a lack of living-wage jobs. Two-thirds of the homeless suffer from chronic or infectious diseases, and 39 percent are mentally ill.

HUD offered one positive spin on the information: When the homeless do hook up with social service organizations offering drug and alcohol treatment and job counseling, a large percentage succeed in finding permanent housing. "Homeless people are locked out of America's prosperity, but we have the key that can let them in," HUD Secretary Andrew Cuomo said. "Assistance programs can replace the nightmare of homelessness with the American dream of a better future."

The "key" to helping the homeless rests in the hands of city governments. But instead of looking for real solutions, politicians all over the country are more concerned with maintaining an image of prosperity. Playing down the homeless problem means finding new ways to "clean up" the homeless, whether by police action or through more subtle maneuvers.

"Quality-of-Life" Violations

New York Mayor Rudy Giuliani has become infamous for his overzealous prosecution of "quality-of-life" violations, ranging from jay-walking to public drinking. Even tourists and wealthy residents have been arrested in the crack-down, but it is the homeless who bear the brunt of Giuliani's law-and-order mentality. In November 1999, he threatened to arrest anyone sleeping in the street, saying "Streets do not exist in civilized societies for the purpose of people sleeping there. Bedrooms are for sleeping."

Giuliani is far from alone. San Francisco Mayor Willie Brown, who promised to address homelessness in a meaningful way in his first campaign in 1995, has earned scathing criticism for his attempts to evict the homeless from Golden Gate Park. During the summer of 1999 the city budget passed with an extra $250,000 allotted for prosecution of quality-of-life offenses. These funds will be used against homeless people charged with infractions like sleeping or urinating in public and possessing open containers of alcohol. Police harassment of the homeless in San Francisco has been stepped up over the past two months, with five times more sleeping-in-public citations issued in March 2000 than in previous months. "[Brown] has given up on doing anything to solve the problem," says Adam Arms, a staff attorney at the San Francisco Coalition for the Homeless. "He's just leaving it to the police to sweep them away so they're out of sight."

Chicago has also taken steps to criminalize the homeless. During the winter of 1999, the city made controversial sweeps of homeless encampments on Lower Wacker Drive, throwing out the belongings of homeless people who had been congregating by the heating vents on the covered downtown roadway. The city then fenced off the places where people had been living.

A "Homeless Removal Program"

Now, in the wake of several highly publicized crimes on the "el" trains, Chicago plans to remove the homeless from late-night public transportation. The city says aid stations will be set up at the end of the all-night Red Line to refer homeless people to shelters and other services. While advocates for the homeless say this aid is a good thing, . . . barring the homeless from getting back on the trains is a gross violation of their civil rights. "They originally announced the policy as a homeless removal program, and that's what it is," says John Donahue, executive director of the Chicago Coalition for the Homeless. "It was only when we began to advocate against it that they started saying they would just be offering services. Well if you're just offering services, you don't need a press conference with the police there, talking about violence on the CTA."

The Coalition for the Homeless is especially incensed at the city's criminalization of homeless people on the trains, given the shooting death of Arthur Earl Hutchinson, a homeless man, earlier in the spring of 2000. Hutchinson was shot by a Chicago police officer outside a train station after he was seen acting erratically on the train; the officer chased Hutchinson into an alley before shooting him, claiming he thought Hutchinson had a weapon. He was found holding a fork.

Matt Wuerker. Reprinted with permission.

Other cities have created similar ways to criminalize their homeless populations. Keeping up military-style operations it perfected during the 1996 Olympics, Atlanta has been conducting regular sweeps to remove people from under downtown bridges. Officials there also distribute photos of homeless people they have labeled "habitual drinkers" to liquor stores. In Tucson, Arizona, city officials have attempted to privatize sidewalks in downtown business districts so business owners can legally deny access to homeless people.

Even efforts by homeless people to improve their situation have been thwarted by city governments and police. When Seattle closed 130 shelter beds on March 31, 2000, the official end of winter, more than 50 homeless people set up their own tent city in a meadow on the south side of the city. Strict rules against alcohol, drugs, fighting and profanity governed the community, and neighbors were impressed with its atmosphere, according to local newspapers. The encampment was on private land owned by a sympathetic landlord, but the city government was determined to close the tents down. Mayor Paul Schell decided to enforce zoning codes that prohibited that many people from sleeping on the owner's land, and threatened to fine him $ 75 a day until the campers were gone. On April 25, the day the fines were to take effect, the campers moved to a new location, where the cycle may start over again. "They're managing to zone the city so the homeless aren't permitted anywhere," says Claude "Cowboy" Nalls, a resident of the tent community. "The only way we can survive is by sticking together like this, but the city wants to disperse us. Then we'll be under viaducts or in the woods, where all kinds of harm can come to you."

More Homeless, Fewer Shelters

Organizing efforts by the homeless may become harder to shun as the dangerous combination of welfare reform, a nationwide affordable housing crunch and more exclusionary shelter plans promises to increase the homeless population.

Employees at shelters around the country say they have seen numbers of homeless people needing shelter go up in direct response to welfare cuts. The effects of welfare reform will continue to snowball over the next few years as people reach their time limit on the public aid rolls. Many people kicked off welfare fail to get any kind of work at all, and those who do succeed in getting jobs are likely to have such low wages that they may still become homeless.

Public housing redevelopment in many cities promises to

put thousands more out on the street. In Chicago, nearly 16,000 units of public housing are slated to be destroyed over the next five years. But numerous studies have shown that enough affordable housing for those who qualify for government subsidies just isn't there. The Chicago public housing plan also includes a get-tough approach on tenants that could leave many with no housing if they have any minor drug violations or are late with their rent.

Likewise, San Francisco has decided to start implementing a policy to make it easier to evict elderly and disabled low-income tenants who "pose a health and safety hazard to their neighbors." The policy stipulates that inspectors can issue tickets to residents at 22 of the agency's assisted-living projects for minor infractions including "tolerance of unhealthy conditions." A one-strike policy for possession of drugs, firearms and even dogs is another part of this plan.

In Silicon Valley, the cradle of out-of-control dot-com wealth, the housing crunch has gotten so bad that even people working two jobs have taken to sleeping on the area's few all-night buses. In February 2000 the *New York Times* reported that even professionals making more than $50,000 a year are turning to homeless shelters. Conditions are similar in the Pacific Northwest. "We have a very overheated economy because of all this high-tech stuff," says Tim Harris, director of the street newspaper *Real Change* in Seattle. "It's getting harder and harder for anyone who's not a yuppie to afford rent anywhere."

While the need for shelters is becoming greater, the number and accessibility of shelter beds continues to decrease. Under San Francisco's new shelter plan, the homeless must pay for their beds. Those on public aid will have the cost deducted from their benefits, signing away all but about $60 of their monthly checks if they stay in the shelter full time. Under the new plan, only 255 of San Francisco's 1,520 shelter beds would be available for people not receiving welfare, even though nearly 70 percent of the more than 14,000 homeless in the city fall into that category. Of those 255 beds, only 50 would be reserved for women. And while the homeless would be effectively paying rent for the shelter, they would have no tenancy rights and would still be subject to the shelters' strict rules. As of early May 2000, it was still unclear whether and how the plan will be implemented, given the intense criticism from the community.

In 1999 Chicago proposed a similar centralized shelter plan. Critics say the plan, which has yet to be implemented, will further decrease the number of people receiving shelter and services. Women who are fleeing domestic abuse—a large segment of the female homeless population—say the centralized intake center would mean their abuser would know exactly where to find them. Undocumented immigrants, already grossly underserved by homeless services, would be even more wary of visiting the centralized centers. "Latino homeless people already face numerous obstacles to getting shelter, because of cultural and language barriers and racism in the shelters," says Jose Landaverde, a leader of the Latino Task Force Against Homelessness in Chicago. "And if they're undocumented they're nervous about being deported. This plan makes it even worse because they are even less likely to go to a shelter if it's not in their neighborhood."

The Need for a Cooperative Model

Most advocates agree that city governments can begin to address the homelessness problem only by turning away from the criminalization approach in favor of a co-operative model involving various sectors of the community. In particular, they say governments should turn to and help finance nonprofit housing, substance abuse treatment, and job training agencies, instead of trying to tackle the problem by themselves.

Thresholds, a city-funded private organization in Chicago that offers intense one-on-one service to the mentally ill, is one group that is taking a proactive approach to homelessness. Advocates also point to church-based programs such as the Night Ministry as effective service providers. Homeless advocates in several major cities were reluctant to name any city programs as being effective in directly fighting homelessness. They say the best things city and state governments are currently doing involve affordable housing programs and tax breaks or subsidies to developers of private low-income housing.

On the national level, lobbying for affordable housing has proven most effective in fighting homelessness. The National Coalition for the Homeless, with members in most major cities, continuously advocates for affordable housing and against criminalization of the homeless. And coalitions of nonprofits like National People's Action (NPA) have made concrete strides in Washington regarding various housing rights. Improvements in the financially troubled Federal Housing Administration loan program is just one area where legislators responded directly to NPA's demands.

Such interest-group pressure is key to influencing the behavior of city governments toward the homeless, says Donahue. Pushing for reform on a national scale puts cities and their policies under a much-needed microscope. "They want to hide the truth about the fact that this hot economy is making more people homeless," he says. "But people are demanding justice."

> *"The mental health system must provide for the occasional involuntary treatment of seriously mentally ill individuals."*

Some of the Homeless Mentally Ill Should Be Treated Involuntarily

E. Fuller Torrey

Beginning in the 1960s, long-term mental patients were released from public psychiatric hospitals back into society—a social experiment referred to as "deinstitutionalization." E. Fuller Torrey claims in the following viewpoint that deinstitutionalization is responsible for the large numbers of mentally ill individuals living on the streets, some of whom pose a threat to public safety. Torrey, a Washington, D.C., psychiatrist and the author of *Out of the Shadows: Confronting America's Mental Illness Crisis*, contends that society must provide hospitalization for the severely mentally ill; furthermore, laws should be reformed to allow for the occasional involuntary commitment of some mentally ill individuals.

As you read, consider the following questions:
1. According to Torrey, why did the idea of deinstitutionalization have appeal across the political spectrum?
2. What percentage of mentally ill patients did not seek psychiatric treatment after being discharged from mental hospitals, as stated by the author?
3. In the author's view, what should be the standard for involuntary commitment?

Reprinted from "Stop the Madness," by E. Fuller Torrey, *The Wall Street Journal*, July 18, 1997 (adapted from the original article in the Summer 1997 issue of the Manhattan Institute's *City Journal*), by permission of the author.

Each year, about 1,000 people in the U.S. are murdered by severely mentally ill people who are not receiving treatment. These killings—about 5% of all homicides nationwide—are a testament to the perversity of deinstitutionalization. The emptying of our public psychiatric hospitals, a massive social experiment involving the release of some 830,000 patients, was undertaken on a multitude of flawed assumptions. It's time to reverse course.

Only a small minority of the mentally ill are violent, but many more are worse off than if they had remained in the hospital. They can be found carrying on animated conversations with themselves in public, living in cardboard boxes or—like one man who lived beneath New York's FDR Drive—training themselves for space missions. They often end up victimized, in jail for misdemeanors, or prematurely dead from accidents, suicide or untreated illnesses.

Seymour Kaplan, a psychiatrist who was one of the pioneers of deinstitutionalization in New York state, later called it the gravest error he ever made. The Empire State, which has released some 90% of its mental patients, typifies the policy's failures.

Perhaps the ultimate symbol is the Keener Men's Shelter. For 75 years it was part of Manhattan State Hospital. As the state emptied the hospital through deinstitutionalization, Keener became a homeless shelter.

When I visited a few years ago, it housed 800 men, 40% of whom were severely mentally ill. Several had been hospital patients in the same building—only then, they got the intensive psychiatric care they needed.

Deinstitutionalization has wreaked havoc on the quality of life, especially in New York City. Recent reductions in crime notwithstanding, New Yorkers still live with the fear that, as one local columnist put it, "from out of the chaos some maniac will emerge to . . . cast you into oblivion."

The presence of even nonviolent mentally ill homeless in the streets and parks creates an inescapable sense of squalor and degradation.

How have things gone so wrong? It is important to realize that the original underpinning for deinstitutionalization was ideology, not science. The idea had appeal across the political spectrum: Liberals found civil libertarian demands for mental patients' "freedom" persuasive, conservatives were happy to cut mental health budgets by shutting down state hospitals.

When deinstitutionalization shifted into high gear in the early 1960s, only one study had been done on the effects of moving severely mentally ill individuals to community living. The 20 schizophrenics in that study, published in England in 1960, did relatively well when moved from a hospital to a supervised community facility.

Virtually every American advocate for deinstitutionalization in the 1960s and '70s cited this paper—and did not mention that the 20 patients had been selected for the experiment because they were functioning at a high level and were able to work, unlike the vast majority of U.S. patients who would be sent packing.

Advocates of deinstitutionalization based their argument mostly on such texts as Erving Goffman's "Asylums" (1961), which asserted that psychiatric patients' abnormal behavior was mostly a consequence not of mental illness but of hospitalization.

Research in the past decade has proved this assumption false: Studies using such techniques as positron emission tomography scans have shown that schizophrenia and manic-depressive illness are physical disorders of the brain, just as Parkinson's disease and multiple sclerosis are. Patients with such illnesses need medications to control their symptoms, which usually get worse without treatment.

Advocates assumed that mentally ill individuals would voluntarily seek psychiatric treatment if they needed it. As it turned out, about half of the patients discharged from psychiatric hospitals did not seek treatment once out of the hospital.

Many of those who suffer from schizophrenia and manic-depressive disorder do not believe themselves to be ill. These untreated individuals constitute most of the mentally ill population who are homeless or in jail, and who commit violent acts. States, meanwhile, shirked their responsibility, in part because the mentally ill were newly eligible for a variety of federal programs.

During the mass exodus of patients from psychiatric hospitals, nobody bothered to ask what was happening to them. Incredibly, despite the vast scale of deinstitutionalization, the federal and state governments never commissioned evaluations of this social experiment, which after all had been launched with virtually no empirical base.

As late as 1981, when deinstitutionalization had been under way for over 15 years, an academic review of research on the subject found only five studies concerned with outcomes, three of which were methodologically flawed.

Helping Those Who Cannot Help Themselves

When people are freezing because they can't be convinced to wear more than shorts in subzero weather, or when they show violent tendencies [that police] officers believe could lead to a tragedy, detaining them overnight on mercy charges seems grossly inadequate. The officers often wish some of those they must watch would commit some offense serious enough to warrant a longer incarceration and a psychological evaluation—which might help them find a way out of the maze.

Scientific advances in diagnosis and treatment have helped many mentally ill people. And many services ranging from soup kitchens to literacy programs are available. But those whose minds are too crippled even to recognize that they are ill are "protected" by current laws from receiving help against their will.

Aimee Howd, *Insight on the News*, September 14, 1998.

During these same years, the National Institute of Mental Health discovered that patients being released from state psychiatric hospitals were not—with only occasional exceptions—receiving after-care.

What can be done to correct this debacle? First, responsibility for mental illness services should be fixed at the state and local levels. This is not something the federal government does well.

Federal funds now being used for mental illness services should be given to the states in block grants, with responsibility should come accountability. State mental illness services should undergo an annual evaluation—carried out by a private contractor—that would partially determine the size of the next federal block grant.

How would mental illness services change? States would doubtless discover that eliminating all state hospital beds is ultimately not cost-effective. A small percentage of seriously mentally ill persons need long-term hospitalization and many more need monitoring to ensure compliance with their treatment regime.

A second, more controversial reform is no less essential: The mental health system must provide for the occasional involuntary treatment of seriously mentally ill individuals. The crux of any commitment law is the conditions it sets for involuntary commitment to be legal.

In many states, patients may be committed only if they can be shown to pose a danger to themselves or others, Courts often interpret this provision very strictly. The standard should not be dangerousness but helplessness. Society has an obligation to save people from degradation, not just death.

Temptation to Accept

A major danger in thinking about the disaster of deinstitutionalization is the temptation to accept it. An entire generation of young adults has grown up seeing homeless mentally ill individuals living on the streets and in the parks.

From their perspective, why shouldn't these people always live there? They are just one more inescapable blight on the urban landscape, along with broken-down cars at the curbs and garbage under the bridges.

It is important for those of us who are older to speak out. We remember when homelessness was rare. We must not accept as inevitable the debacle of deinstitutionalization and its consequences.

We made this problem and we can correct it.

"In some urban areas, homelessness itself is interpreted as proof of 'grave disability,' creating the justification to drug homeless people against their will."

The Homeless Mentally Ill Should Not Be Treated Involuntarily

Chance Martin

In the subsequent viewpoint, Chance Martin contends that involuntary outpatient commitment—which forces treatment or hospital confinement on unwilling individuals—is an attack on the civil rights of the mentally ill. The homeless mentally ill should not be drugged or locked up against their will; instead, they should be offered voluntary, community-based mental health treatment. Martin is the editor of *Street Sheet*, a publication of the National Coalition on Homelessness, in San Francisco. He has experienced homelessness and forced treatment due to severe psychiatric disability.

As you read, consider the following questions:
1. What are the different types of involuntary outpatient commitment, according to the author?
2. In the author's view, who are the victims of involuntary commitment?
3. How were the mentally ill treated during the Holocaust, as stated by Martin?

Reprinted from "Promoting Stigma," by Chance Martin, November 1999, at http://aspin.asu.edu/hpn/archives/Nov99/0195.html, by permission of the author.

After decades of neglect, our state legislature is being aggressively lobbied to restore California's mental health system. All of the proposed treatment enhancements and services are desperately needed and would be welcome, with one exception—an attack on the civil rights of mentally disabled people called involuntary outpatient commitment.

Involuntary outpatient commitment is court-mandated medication compliance. It can mean a person is court-ordered to keep regular clinic appointments to receive long-lasting injections of powerful psychiatric drugs. The consequences of non-compliance are hospital commitment and forced drugging. These proposed legal provisions are termed "assisted treatment."

The Victims of Involuntary Commitment

In practice, its primary victims are poor and homeless people, particularly African-American men. In some urban areas, homelessness itself is interpreted as proof of "grave disability," creating the justification to drug homeless people against their will. In states where this policy is law, forced medication coupled with a lack of medical supervision has led to deaths due to toxic levels of psychiatric medication.

At New York City's Bellevue hospital, a pilot study testing the viability of involuntary outpatient commitment failed to support its advocates' claims. A three year study of its relative effectiveness found no statistically significant differences between the experimental group, a control group, and those who discontinued treatment in the areas of re-hospitalization, arrests, violence, symptomatology, or quality of life. It concluded: "There is no indication that, overall, the court order for outpatient commitment produces better outcomes for clients or the community than enhanced services alone."

Alarmingly, it also noted that the court procedures themselves became perfunctory, and accountability was so lacking that renewal orders frequently occurred without a formal hearing, despite the fact that "the court order itself had no discernible added value in producing better outcomes."

The betrayal of the deinstitutionalization movement in California only became apparent when the state-funded community-based mental health services to replace the snake pits were themselves facing extinction. Now we are faced with a proposal to criminalize an entire community of people based on disability. Disability isn't a choice; it's something each of us learns to accommodate as best we can. We need to ask ourselves: How many violent acts committed by untreated mentally ill people, however sensationalized, might have been prevented if a comprehensive range of voluntary, culturally appropriate community mental health services had been available?

The Problems with Involuntary Outpatient Commitment

• Singles out a class of individuals and mandates submission to forced psychiatric

• Forced treatment based upon mental diagnosis infringes upon the individual's civil liberties

• Expansion of involuntary commitment laws to cover outpatient commitment is a direct attack on and leads to the imposition of forced treatment on individuals who do not present a danger to themselves or others

• Outpatient commitment interferes with a person's right to choice. People recover when they have choice among alternative treatments and services, when they are empowered to make their own decisions and take responsibility for their lives, and when they are offered hope

• The ability for individuals with mental illness to exercise their right to refuse treatment is non-existent in the confines of Involuntary Outpatient Commitment

Elaine Sutton Mbionwu, *StopAbuse.net*, January 30, 2000.

A look at twentieth century history gives the best illustration of how far stigmatization, scapegoating and hate can go when misrepresented as scientific authority.

Eugenics originated as a subdiscipline of psychiatry here in the United States. The first compulsory sterilization laws in Germany were modeled on American sterilization laws enacted a decade before. In the three years from 1941–1943, over 42,000 Americans were sterilized under the Model Eugenical Sterilization Law.

California led the nation with over 10,000 forced sterilizations (mostly persons of color). The "mental diseases" targeted by this law were "insane," "feeble-minded," "epileptics," and "idiots."

The Holocaust's first victims were "mentally ill" people. The first extermination facilities were operated by psychiatrists, who then trained the SS how to use them. In a society where ruling authority was maintained in the name of a higher "biological" principle, psychiatrists weren't ordered to murder people, they were simply empowered to do so by their government, so they did. In 1941, 90,000 German psychiatric inmates were murdered, 71,000 in gas chambers at psychiatric institutions.

If our generation remembers no other lesson, we must remember that no supposed biological marker—no stigma—is reason enough to deny anyone's liberty. We must support fully funded, community-based, VOLUNTARY mental health treatment before we consider discarding another person's self-determination.

If it isn't voluntary, it isn't treatment.

| *"Private charity is more likely to focus on short-term emergency assistance than on long-term dependence."*

Private Charities Can Help the Homeless

Michael Tanner

Private charities, not government welfare programs, are best equipped to deal with social problems such as homelessness, contends Michael Tanner in the viewpoint that follows. Because charities promote personal responsibility and offer individualized attention, he maintains, they are extremely successful in helping the poor regain self-sufficiency. Tanner is director of health and welfare studies at the Cato Institute, a nonpartisan public policy research foundation that promotes limited government, individual liberty, and peace.

As you read, consider the following questions:
1. Why are private charities better equipped than welfare programs to give individualized attention to the poor, as stated by Tanner?
2. According to the author, why is it easier for private charities than for government to demand that recipients change their behavior?
3. What do recipients learn from private charity, in Tanner's view?

Reprinted from "Civil Society to the Rescue," by Michael Tanner, *CATO: This Just In*, July 1, 1997, by permission of the author.

Those who believe that only government can solve the problems of poverty should take note of a remarkable anniversary. Gospel Rescue Ministries, one of the nation's most successful private charitable institutions, turned 90 in May 1997. Since 1907—long before presidential summits on volunteerism—they have been helping the poorest Americans get off the streets, find jobs and rebuild their lives.

The D.C. branch of the organization operates from a converted crack house in Chinatown. Relying on volunteers and private contributions—not government money—the ministry operates a 150-man shelter, soup kitchen, food bank, and drug treatment center. The ministry addresses its clients' needs for more than food and shelter: It provides education, job placement assistance and spiritual advice.

Unlike government welfare programs, the ministry operates on the principle that no one should receive something for nothing. Therefore, the homeless must pay $3.00 a night or agree to perform one hour of work on the premises in exchange for lodging.

By insisting that the poor take responsibility for their lives, the ministry has been extraordinarily successful in helping its clients put their lives back together. For example, nearly two out of three of the addicts completing its drug treatment program remain drug free. But a government-run drug treatment center just three blocks away has only a 10 percent success rate, although it spends nearly 20 times as much per client.

Gospel Rescue Ministries is a tiny fraction of American charitable efforts. Americans contribute more than $125 billion annually to charity. More than 85 percent of all adult Americans make some charitable contribution each year. In addition, about half of all American adults perform volunteer work: more than 20 billion hours in 1991. Translated into dollars, the value of that volunteer work was more than $176 billion. Americans' charitable contributions total more than $300 billion per year.

More Successful than Government Welfare

Private charities have been more successful than government welfare has at actually helping people for several reasons.

First, private charities are able to give individual attention in ways that governments can't. Government regulations must be designed to treat all similarly situated recipients alike. Most government programs provide cash or other goods and services without any attempt to differentiate between recipients. The sheer size of government programs works against individualization. As one welfare case worker lamented, "With 125 cases it's hard to remember that they're all human beings. Sometimes they're just a number."

Reprinted by permission of Chuck Asay and Creators Syndicate.

In her excellent book, *Tyranny of Kindness,* Theresa Funiciello, a former welfare mother, describes the dehumanizing world of the government welfare system—a system in which regulations and bureaucracy rule all else. It is a system in which illiterate homeless people with mental illnesses are handed 17-page forms to fill out, women nine months pregnant are told to verify their pregnancy, and a woman who was raped is told she is ineligible for benefits because she can't list the baby's father on the required form. It is a world totally unable to adjust to the slightest deviation from the bureaucratic norm.

A Safety Net, Not a Way of Life

Second, private charity is more likely to focus on short-term emergency assistance than on long-term dependence. Private charity provides a safety net, not a way of life. Moreover, it is far easier for private charities than for government to demand that the poor change their behavior: Governments are often hamstrung when they require recipients to stop using alcohol or drugs, look for a job, or avoid pregnancy. Private charities are much more likely than government programs to offer individual counseling and monitoring rather than simply cut a check.

Finally, and perhaps most important, private charity requires a different attitude on the part of both recipients and donors. Recipients learn that private charity is not an entitlement but a gift carrying reciprocal obligations. Donors learn that private charity demands they become directly involved. There is no compassion in spending someone else's money—even for a good cause. True compassion depends on personal involvement.

Thus private charity is ennobling for everyone involved, both those who give and those who receive. Government welfare ennobles no one.

Still in doubt? Consider this: if you had $10,000 available that you wanted to use to help the poor, would you give it to the government to help fund welfare, or would you donate it to a group like Gospel Rescue Ministries?

"[Private] charities are not prepared to take on a sizable new population of people in need."

Private Charities Cannot Help All of the Homeless

Joseph P. Shapiro and Jennifer Seter

In the subsequent viewpoint, *U.S. News & World Report* writers Joseph P. Shapiro and Jennifer Seter explain why private charities are not equipped to deal with homelessness, poverty, and other social problems. According to the authors, charities simply do not have the financial resources to compensate for recent cuts in federal safety net programs—which have created a burgeoning needy population. Moreover, claim the authors, evidence suggests that private donors are not willing or able to give enough money to support the needy.

As you read, consider the following questions:

1. Why did the government first initiate a social safety net, according to the authors?
2. What percentage of charities' funding comes from the government, claim Shapiro and Seter?
3. According to the authors, what was the golden age of "neighborhood helpfulness"?

If Congress and the White House both want to cut spending for social programs, who will house the homeless, feed the hungry, care for the sick and help the poor? With many states and cities facing their own budget crunches, [former] House Speaker Newt Gingrich says private charities should pick up much of the burden. "I believe in a social safety net, but I think that it's better done by churches and by synagogues and by volunteers," Gingrich told an interviewer.

In fact, it is highly doubtful that charities could pick up all or even most of the slack from the $76 billion to $450 billion in spending cuts now being proposed by Democrats and Republicans in Washington. The federal government, after all, began weaving a social safety net because states and cities, not to mention churches, synagogues and volunteers, could not cope with the Great Depression, urbanization, increased mobility, runaway health care costs, a swelling population and a declining sense of community in America.

Since the 1960s, private charities have become one of government's chief service providers. They are favored for their efficiency, and tax money has enabled them to serve more people. Nationally, charities now get about 30 percent of their funding from government, and many programs get more than half their money from government. Some, such as nursing homes and orphanages, can rely on government for at least 75 percent of their funding.

Not Prepared to Take on More Needy

A look at the Singer Transitional Residence, a long-term shelter, and other social programs affiliated with the Jewish Federation of Metropolitan Chicago shows why charities are not prepared to take on a sizable new population of people in need.

The Chicago federation, the nation's 67th-largest charity, supports cradle-to-grave programs—from therapy for babies of crack-addicted mothers to subsidized housing for the elderly. In 1994, it received $23 million in government funds and raised an additional $27 million to pay for social-spending programs by its affiliated charities. The Singer shelter pays

65 percent of its total costs—from food to night staff— with public moneys. (President Clinton proposed eliminating the shelter's key federal grant.) "It doesn't take much rocket science to figure out that if the resources at our disposal are cut, we will serve fewer people," says the federation's Joel Carp.

The belief that charities can take over from government is rooted in two myths:

Myth 1: Charities Provide a Private Social Safety Net

Federal and state transportation grants paid for the $36,000, dark-blue van, one of 19 belonging to the Council for Jewish Elderly, that picks up 80-year-old Beatrice Glaberson every morning and takes her to an adult day-care center in Rogers Park. The program provides Glaberson with intellectual stimulation, which has helped her recover from a stroke. "It gives you something to do," she says, "instead of sitting at home, watching television, playing solitaire and eating candy."

Glaberson's own day-care bill is largely paid by Medicaid. Chicago's 469-bed Mount Sinai Hospital, which is affiliated with the Jewish Federation, receives less than 1 percent of its funds from private donors, and 80 percent of its patients are on public health insurance.

Myth 2: A Golden Age of Charity Can Be Rekindled

Before the New Deal, there was a golden age of "neighborhood helpfulness," argues David Beito, an assistant professor of history at the University of Alabama. "When there was an accident in a plant, workers would all contribute to help the family," he says. "Today, people don't feel a need to do that. They think, 'I pay taxes for that. There's a program to take care of that.'" Reducing the size of government, Gingrich and others believe, will rekindle American generosity.

University of Pennsylvania history Prof. Michael Katz, however, says government has long supported the needy. The 13 original Colonies provided public relief, he says, and

Private Charities Receive Government Funding

Private charity isn't entirely private, and hasn't been for decades. In the 1960s, when the government greatly expanded its services to the poor, it turned much of the money—and the responsibility—over to those assumed to have an expertise in helping. As a result, 63% of Catholic Charities USA's $1.9 billion annual budget last year consisted of money from federal, state and local governments, including grants from eight different federal agencies. In return, the charity provided such services as battered-women's shelters, day care, home care for the elderly, foster care and adoption services, employment training, services for the homeless and assistance for people with AIDS. Most other large charities concerned with the poor (as opposed to non-profit cultural or advocacy groups, which are sometimes also called charities) get somewhat less government money than the Catholic group, but the average probably still exceeds 31% of their total annual budgets. According to Alan Abramson of the Aspen Institute, the congressional cuts could cost American for-the-poor charities as much as $70 billion during the next seven years. . . .

The Coalition for the Homeless in New York City, which serves 750 dinners a night—a bowl of chicken stew, an orange, fruit juice and a piece of bread—says funding for that program may drop a third.

David Van Biema et al., *Time*, December 4, 1995.

his study of welfare in Buffalo in the 1890s found that up to 75 percent of the programs were government funded.

If government has played a larger role in welfare than Gingrich supposes, Katz wonders if private donors are as ready to assume more of the burden as the House leader thinks. Experts dispute whether contributions to charities have gone up or down slightly in the past few years. But between 1963 and 1993, charitable giving soared from $70 billion to $126 billion, adjusted for inflation, according to the American Association of Fund-Raising Counsel. And Robert Bothwell of the National Committee for Responsive Philanthropy says some 30,000 new groups are formed each year "to deal with new issues and problems."

Gingrich has suggested more-generous tax deductions to

spur people to give more to charity. But if it took 30 years for charitable giving to increase by $56 billion, it is hard to imagine that private donors can come up with at least $76 billion to take up the slack from Uncle Sam. Says Katz: "To think Americans will spend a tax cut on the poor, instead of at the mall, is a very generous interpretation of American character."

Periodical Bibliography

The following articles have been selected to supplement the diverse views presented in this chapter. Addresses are provided for periodicals not indexed in the *Readers' Guide to Periodical Literature*, the *Alternative Press Index*, the *Social Sciences Index*, or the *Index to Legal Periodicals and Books*.

Alice Callaghan	"Private Security Bores in on the Homeless," *Los Angeles Times*, November 22, 1999.
Stacey Chambers	"How Any Person on the Street Can Help a Street Person," *Humanist*, January/February 1999.
Ronald W. Fagan	"Deserving of Hostility or Compassion?" *San Diego Union-Tribune*, March 3, 1999.
Maria Foscarinis	"Stop Punishing the Homeless," *Christian Science Monitor*, December 9, 1999.
Richard Goldstein	"Sanctioned Sadism: Why the Right Needs the Homeless," *Village Voice*, December 14, 1999.
Bob Herbert	"Blueprint for Tragedy," *The New York Times*, November 1, 1999.
Bob Herbert	"A Cold Wind Blows," *The New York Times*, January 24, 2000.
Aimee Howd	"Trapped Between Law and Madness," *Insight on the News*, September 14, 1998.
Rael Jean Isaac and D.J. Jaffe	"Committed to Help: Toward Rational Commitment Laws," *National Review*, January 29, 1996.
Carla Jacobs and E. Fuller Torrey	"It's Time We Help California's Helpless," *San Diego Union-Tribune*, February 16, 2000.
Jodie Morse	"Cracking Down on the Homeless," *Time*, December 20, 1999.
Evelyn Nieves	"Is a Crackdown the Answer?" *The New York Times Upfront*, January 31, 2000.
Karla Pollitt	"Home Discomforts," *Nation*, January 24, 2000.
David Van Biema et al.	"Society: Can Charity Fill the Gap? Groups That Help the Poor Are Bracing for a Double Hardship: Surging Need and Federal Budget Cuts," *Time*, December 4, 1995.

For Further Discussion

Chapter 1

1. Based on what you have read in this chapter, how prevalent is homelessness? Does the problem of homelessness merit serious concern? Give specific reasons for your answer.

2. The *Washington Spectator* argues that homelessness is a societal problem. In contrast, C.J. Carnacchio contends that homelessness is not society's concern. Whose argument is more convincing, and why? In your opinion, is society responsible for ending homelessness?

3. What is the stereotype of a homeless person? How do the viewpoints by Yvonne M. Vissing, and Eugene M. Lewit and Linda Schuurmann Baker challenge this stereotype?

Chapter 2

1. Based on your reading of this chapter, is homelessness voluntary, or do circumstances force people into homelessness? Provide evidence from the viewpoints to support your answer.

2. List the economic and noneconomic factors that contribute to homelessness, as mentioned by the authors in this chapter. Which list is more significant, in your view? Why?

3. Of the causes of homelessness discussed in this chapter, which is the most serious, in your view? Support your arguments with specific examples from the viewpoints. Can you think of other possible causes of homelessness not mentioned in this chapter?

Chapter 3

1. Andrew Cuomo asserts that the federal government should play a strong role in providing affordable housing options for the poor and the homeless. Howard Husock, on the other hand, maintains that the federal government's role in providing affordable housing should be extremely minimal. What reasons do Cuomo and Husock give to support their arguments? Whose case is more persuasive, and why?

2. List the advantages and disadvantages of housing vouchers, as discussed in this chapter. Do the advantages outweigh the disadvantages, or vice versa? Why?

3. Based on what you have read in this chapter, what combination of housing options would best help the homeless? Explain your answer.

Chapter 4

1. David Brooks contends that local governments should crack down on street vagrants by arresting them if they refuse offers of shelter and by requiring them to work for their shelter. According to Karl Lydersen, however, these measures infringe upon the civil rights of the homeless. Whose argument do you agree with, and why? What civil rights do the homeless have, in your opinion?

2. Based on your reading of the viewpoints by E. Fuller Torrey and Chance Martin, is it acceptable for society to force the homeless mentally ill to obtain treatment? Why or why not?

3. Michael Tanner argues that private charities are the best way to help the homeless; Joseph P. Shapiro and Jennifer Seter, in contrast, claim that private charities by themselves are not equipped to help the homeless. Compare the authors' use of statistics. Which viewpoint uses statistics more effectively? Why?

Organizations and Websites

The editors have compiled the following list of organizations and websites concerned with the issues debated in this book. The descriptions are derived from materials provided by the organizations themselves. All have publications or information available for interested readers. The list was compiled on the date of publication of the present volume; the information provided here may change. Be aware that many organizations take several weeks or longer to respond to inquiries, so allow as much time as possible.

Cato Institute
1000 Massachusetts Ave. NW, Washington, DC 20001
(202) 842-0200 • fax: (202) 842-4390
e-mail: librarian@cato.org • website: www.cato.org

A libertarian public policy research foundation, the Cato Institute opposes rent control, restrictive zoning laws, and other regulations of the housing market. It advocates vouchers to solve the problems of homelessness. Its publications include the book *Zoning, Rent Control and Affordable Housing* and the monthly *Policy Report* and *Cato Journal*.

Coalition for the Homeless
89 Chambers St., New York, NY 10007
(212) 964-5900, ext. 113 • fax: (212) 964-1303
e-mail: cfthomeless@aol.com
website: www.coalitionforhomeless.org/

The coalition is both an advocacy organization that addresses issues of homelessness and a service provider to homeless people in New York City. It uses litigation, lobbying, organizing, and public education to solve the problem of homelessness. It publishes results of its research on the homeless in its reports *Losing the War Home: Privatization and the Municipal Shelter System* and *The Second Wave: The Looming Homeless Crisis in the Post-Entitlement Era*.

Co-operative Housing Association of Ontario (CHAO)
2 Berkeley St., Suite 207, Toronto, ON M5A 2W3 Canada
(800) 268-2537 • fax: (416) 366-3876

CHAO is a provincial housing advocacy group that works with other housing and homeless organizations throughout Ontario to develop educational and political campaigns. It maintains a housing research library with resource materials on housing issues in Canada and around the world. CHAO commissions and publishes studies on a variety of housing issues. Its publications include the monthly *Dispatches* and *Co-op Memo*, the biweekly *Resource Group Memo*, the quarterly newsletter *Co-op Bulletin*, and the semiannual *Cross Sections*.

Habitat for Humanity International
121 Habitat St., Americus, GA 31709
(229) 924-6935
e-mail: publicinfo@hfhi.org • website: www.habitat.org

HFHI is a nonprofit, nondenominational Christian housing organization that helps people in need of shelter to build simple, affordable houses.

The Heritage Foundation
214 Massachusetts Ave. NE, Washington, DC 20002-4999
(202) 546-4400 • fax: (202) 546-8328
website: www.heritage.org

The foundation is a conservative think tank that conducts research on public policy. An advocate of free enterprise and limited government, it argues that the free market can best meet the housing needs of the homeless. Its periodic publications *Backgrounder* and *Issues Bulletin* often deal with homelessness and related issues.

Homes for the Homeless (HFH)
36 Cooper Square, 6th Floor, New York, NY 10003
(212) 529-5252 • fax: (212) 529-7698
e-mail: info@homesforthehomeless.com
website: www2.homesforthehomeless.com

HFH strives to reduce homelessness by providing families with the education and training they need to build independent lives. Participating families are housed in one of four residential educational training centers in New York City, where they learn job, literacy, and parenting skills. Participants are also counseled on substance abuse and domestic violence. HFH publishes the reports *Homelessness: The Foster Care Connection*, *The New Poverty: A Generation of Homeless Families*, *An American Family Myth: Every Child at Risk*, and *Job Readiness: Crossing the Threshold from Homelessness to Employment*.

Housing Assistance Council (HAC)
1025 Vermont Ave. NW, Suite 606, Washington, DC 20005
(202) 842-8600 • fax: (202) 347-3441
website: www.ruralhousing.org

The council conducts research projects and provides loans, information, and technical assistance on homelessness and low-income housing developments to rural housing agencies. It publishes the biweekly newsletter *HAC News*, the bimonthly newsletter *State Action Memorandum*, and fact sheets on rural homelessness.

National Alliance for the Mentally Ill (NAMI)

Colonial Place Three, 2107 Wilson Blvd., Suite 300, Arlington, VA 22201-3042
1-800-950-6264 • fax: (703) 524-9094
website: www.nami.org

The mission of NAMI is "to eradicate mental illnesses and improve the quality of life of those affected by these diseases." Some of NAMI's goals are to be the primary source of information on all aspects of mental illness, to educate the general public on mental illness, to assist educators and caregivers in incorporating current research into their mental illness practices, and to obtain government resources to help those with mental illness, including those who are homeless.

National Alliance to End Homelessness, Inc.

1518 K St. NW, Suite 206, Washington, DC 20005
(202) 638-1526 • fax: (202) 638-4664
e-mail: naeh@naeh.org • website: www.naeh.org

The alliance is composed of state and local nonprofit agencies, corporations, and individuals who provide housing and services to homeless people. Its goal is to end homelessness by changing federal policy and by helping its local members serve more homeless people. It publishes the newsletter *Alliance*, the report *Web of Failure: The Relationship Between Foster Care and Homelessness*, and the book *What You Can Do to Help the Homeless*.

National Coalition for Homeless Veterans (NCHV)

333½ Pennsylvania Ave. SE, Washington, DC 20003-1148
(202) 546-1969 • fax: (202) 546-2063
e-mail: nchv@nchv.org • website: www.hnchv.org

The NCHV, founded by a group of service providers to homeless veterans, serves as a liaison between community groups and branches of the federal government. It works to educate the public and shape government policy on homelessness. Its publications include the *Report to the Nation*. Fact sheets on homeless veterans and testimony concerning federal legislation affecting the homeless are provided on the organization's website.

National Coalition for the Homeless

1012 Fourteenth St., NW, Suite 600, Washington, DC 20005-3410
(202) 737-6444 • fax: (202) 737-6445
website: http://nch.ari.net

The National Coalition for the Homeless is a national advocacy network of activists, homeless persons, service providers, and others committed to ending homelessness through public education, policy advocacy, grassroots organizing, and technical assistance. It lobbies for government programs to help the homeless, conducts research, and works as a clearinghouse on information about the homeless. It publishes the monthly newsletter *Safety Network* and many pamphlets and reports, including *Shredding the Safety Network: The Contract with America's Impact on Poor and Homeless People.*

National Law Center on Homelessness and Poverty

1411 K St. NW, Suite 1400, Washington, DC 20005
(202) 638-2535 • fax: (202) 628-2737
e-mail: nlchp@nlchp.org • website: www.nlchp.org

The mission of the National Law Center on Homelessness and Poverty is to protect the rights of homeless people and to implement solutions to end homelessness in America. To achieve its mission, the center pursues three main strategies: impact litigation, policy advocacy, and public education. It regards homelessness as an effect of the shortage of affordable housing, insufficient wages, and inadequate social services. The center publishes the monthly newsletter *In Just Times.*

National Resource Center on Homelessness and Mental Health

345 Delaware Ave., Delmar, NY 12054
(800) 444-7415 • fax: (518) 439-7612
e-mail: hch@prainc.com • website: www.prainc.com/hch

The center provides comprehensive information about the treatment, social services, and housing needs of homeless persons with severe mental illness. Its extensive database of publications includes the quarterly *Access* and the resource guide *National Organizations Concerned with Mental Health, Housing, and Homelessness.*

National Runaway Switchboard (NRS)

3080 N. Lincoln Ave., Chicago, IL 60657
(773) 880-9860 • fax: (773) 929-5150
crisis line: (800) 621-4000
e-mail: info@nrscrisisline.org • website: www.nrscrisisline.org

The NRS operates a confidential hotline for runaway youth, teens in crisis, and concerned friends and family members. All services are free and available 24 hours a day. NRS services include: crisis intervention; message relay between runaways and their parents or legal guardians; referrals to community-based resources, such as counseling, support groups, alternative housing, and health care; and the Home Free program, in partnership with Greyhound Buslines, which helps runaways return to their families.

National Student Campaign Against Hunger and Homelessness
29 Temple Pl., 4th Floor, Boston, MA 02111
(617) 292-4823 • fax: (617) 292-8057
e-mail: nscahh@aol.com • website: www.pirg.org/nscahh/

The campaign trains students to improve or create service programs to meet the needs of the hungry and homeless in their communities. It also holds workshops and conferences to educate people about the antipoverty movement. Its publications include the newsletter *Students Making a Difference* and various fact sheets. It also offers catalogs of academic courses, internships, and volunteer opportunities across the nation.

U.S. Department of Housing and Urban Development (HUD)
Office of Homelessness, 451 Seventh St. SW, Room 9206
Washington, DC 20410
(202) 708-4432
website: www.hud.gov

HUD is the federal agency responsible for housing programs and the development and preservation of neighborhoods. For the past several years, it has worked to encourage the private housing market to provide affordable housing for all. The Office of Special Needs Assistance Programs, under the aegis of the Stewart B. McKinney Act, funds a variety of homeless assistance programs. HUD publishes the report *Priority Home! The Federal Plan to Break the Cycle of Homelessness* and several other reports about affordable housing and homelessness.

Websites

Directory of Local Homeless Service Organizations
http://nch.ari.net/local/local.html

This website, sponsored by the National Coalition for the Homeless, contains searchable listings of local direct service providers to the homeless.

Homeless People's Network

http://aspin.asu.edu/hpn/

The discussion list provides a forum for homeless and formerly homeless people to express their views. Those interested in homelessness can read archived postings.

Homeless Women's Network

www.speakeasy.org/hwn/

This website is aimed in part at giving homeless or formerly homeless women and youth the skills to use technology in accessing resources.

International Homelessness Homepage

http://csf.colorado.edu/homeless/

This website index contains links to more than five hundred Internet resources including discussion list archives and articles on the homeless.

Bibliography of Books

G. John M. Abbarno   *The Ethics of Homelessness: Philosophical Perspectives*. Atlanta: Rodopi, 1999.

Nels Anderson   *On Hobos and Homelessness*. Chicago: University of Chicago Press, 1998.

Gregg Barak   *Gimme Shelter*. New York: Praeger, 1991.

Alice S. Baum and Donald W. Burnes   *A Nation in Denial: The Truth About Homelessness*. Boulder, CO: Westview Press, 1993.

Joel Blau   *The Visible Poor: Homelessness in the United States*. New York: Oxford University Press, 1992.

Tina S. Bolnik and Jamie Pastor Bolnik   *Living at the Edge of the World: A Teenager's Survival in the Tunnels of Grand Central Station*. New York: St. Martin's Press, 2000.

Namkee G. Choi   *Homeless Families with Children: A Subjective Experience of Homelessness*. New York: Springer, 1999.

Jodi Cobb et al.   *The Way Home: Ending Homelessness in America*. New York: H.N. Abrams, 1999.

Deborah R. Connolly   *Homeless Mothers: Face to Face with Women and Poverty*. Minneapolis: University of Minnesota Press, 2000.

Kevin Cwayna   *Knowing Where the Fountains Are: Stories and Stark Realities of Homeless Youth*. Minneapolis: Deaconess Press, 1993.

Gerald P. Daly   *Homeless: Policies, Strategies, and Lives on the Street*. New York: Routledge, 1996.

Robert R. Desjarlais   *Shelter Blues: Sanity and Selfhood Among the Homeless*. Philadelphia: University of Pennsylvania Press, 1997.

Herbert J. Gans   *The War Against the Poor: The Underclass and Antipoverty Policy*. New York: BasicBooks, 1995.

Irene Glasser   *Homelessness in Global Perspective*. New York: G.K. Hall, 1994.

Mary Jo Huth and Talmadge Wright, eds.   *International Critical Perspectives on Homelessness*. Westport, CT: Praeger, 1997.

Interagency Council on the Homeless   *Outcasts on Main Street: Report of the Federal Task Force on Homelessness and Severe Mental Illness*. 1992. Available from National Resource Center on Homelessness and Mental Illness, Policy Research Associates, 262 Delaware Ave., Delmar, NY 12054.

Rael Jean Isaac and Virginia C. Armat	*Madness in the Streets: How Psychiatry and the Law Abandoned the Mentally Ill.* New York: Free Press, 1990.
Karleen Jackson	*Family Homelessness: More than Simply a Lack of Housing.* New York: Garland, 2000.
Christopher Jencks	*The Homeless.* Cambridge, MA: Harvard University Press, 1994.
Elliot Liebow	*Tell Them Who I Am: The Lives of Homeless Women.* New York: Free Press, 1993.
Dale Maharidge	*The Last Great American Hobo.* Rocklin, CA: Prima Publishing, 1993.
Lawrence M. Mead	*The New Politics of Poverty: The Nonworking Poor in America.* New York: Basic Books, 1992.
Eungjun Min, ed.	*Reading the Homeless: The Media's Image of Homeless Culture.* Westport, CT: Praeger, 1999.
Margaret Morton	*The Tunnel.* New Haven, CT: Yale University Press, 1995.
National Coalition for the Homeless	*Shredding the Safety Net: The Contract with America's Impact on Poor and Homeless People.* December 1994.
Margery G. Nichelason	*Homeless or Hopeless?* Minneapolis: Lerner Publications, 1994.
Ralph DaCosta Nunez	*The New Poverty: Homeless Families in America.* New York: Insight Books, 1996.
Brendan O'Flaherty	*Making Room: The Economics of Homelessness.* Cambridge, MA: Harvard University Press, 1996.
Joanne Passaro	*The Unequal Homeless: Men on the Streets, Women in Their Place.* New York: Routledge, 1996.
Melanie Smith Percy	*"Not Just a Shelter Kid": How Homeless Children Find Solace.* New York: Garland, 1997.
Peter H. Rossi	*Down and Out in America: The Origins of Homelessness.* Chicago: University of Chicago Press, 1989.
Michael Rowe	*Crossing the Border: Encounters Between Homeless People and Outreach Workers.* Berkeley: University of California Press, 1999.
Paul G. Shane	*What About America's Homeless Children?: Hide and Seek.* Thousand Oaks, CA: Sage Publications, 1996.
David A. Snow and Leon Anderson	*Down on Their Luck: A Study of Homeless Street People.* Berkeley and Los Angeles: University of California Press, 1993.

Thomas Szasz | *Cruel Compassion: Psychiatric Control of Society's Unwanted.* New York: Wiley, 1994.

E. Fuller Torrey | *Out of the Shadows: Confronting America's Mental Illness Crisis.* New York: Wiley, 1997.

Yvonne M. Vissing | *Out of Sight, Out of Mind: Homeless Children and Families in Small-Town America.* Lexington: University Press of Kentucky, 1996.

David Wagner | *Checkerboard Square: Culture and Resistance in a Homeless Community.* Boulder, CO: Westview Press, 1993.

Les B. Whitbeck and Dan R. Hoyt | *Nowhere to Grow: Homeless and Runaway Adolescents and Their Families.* New York: Aldine de Gruyer, 1999.

Richard W. White Jr. | *Rude Awakenings: What the Homeless Crisis Tells Us.* San Francisco: ICS Press, 1992.

Jennifer Wolch and Michael Dear | *Malign Neglect: Homelessness in an American City.* San Francisco: Jossey-Bass, 1993.

James D. Wright | *Address Unknown: The Homeless in America.* New York: Aldine de Gruyter, 1989.

Susan Yeich | *The Politics of Ending Homelessness.* Lanham, MD: University Press of America, 1994.

Index

accessory apartments, 108–109
Aid to Families with
  Dependent Children
  (AFDC), 53
  see also welfare reform
alcohol abuse. *See* substance
  abuse
America (magazine), 28
American Civil Liberties
  Union (ACLU), 27
American Prospect (magazine),
  103
Anderson, Richard, 70, 71
Arms, Adam, 144
Asylums (Goffman), 152

Baker, Linda Schuurmann, 39
Barrett, Nicole, 138
Becharov, Douglas J., 53
Beito, David, 165
Berry, Kim, 123
Boden, Paul, 13
Boston Globe (newspaper), 19
Bothwell, Robert, 166
British Columbia Ministry of
  Social Development and
  Economic Security, 129
Brooks, David, 137
Brosch, Eric, 12
Brown, Willie, 144
Browne, Anthony, 45
Buchmeyer, Jerry, 114
Burleson, Bruce, 63
Burnam, M. Audrey, 26

Carnacchio, C.J., 23
Carp, Joel, 165
Census Bureau, U.S.
  on homeless population, 24
Center for Poverty Solutions,
  54

charities
  can best help the homeless,
    159–62
  con, 163–67
child care
  as barrier to employment,
    57–58
children
  educational effects of
    homelessness on, 35–36
  homelessness is a problem
    among, 39–44
  of homeless parents, 22
  poverty rate among, 37
  as stabilizing factor for
    women, 50
  substance abuse and
    homelessness among, 81
Cisneros, Henry G., 72, 113
City Homes, 107
Clinton, Bill, 19, 53, 94, 115,
  165
Clinton, Hillary, 138, 139
Cohen, Warren, 13
community-based development
  organizations, 105
Cousar, Gloria, 121
crime
  as cause of homelessness, 26
  mentally ill homeless as
    victims of, 73–74
Cuomo, Andrew, 21, 91, 143

Dallas Morning News
  (newspaper), 116
deinstitutionalization, 150
  has affected quality of life in
    cities, 151
  is a contributing factor to
    homelessness, 65, 75–77
  origins of, 151–53

reasons for failure of, 152–53
Dolbeare, Cushing, 20
domestic violence
  as cause of homelessness,
    84–87
    research on, 86
  and homelessness among
    women, 43–44
  and rural homelessness, 36
Donahue, John, 144, 149
Drake, Paris, 138
drug abuse. *See* substance abuse
Dworkin, Julie, 53

Economist, The (magazine), 125,
  140
emergency services
  increase in demand for, 30
employment
    barriers, 57–58
      among mentally ill, 73
eugenics, 156–57
Evans, Cynthia, 120, 121

families
  homeless
    numbers of, 41
    welfare reform has increased
      numbers of, 69–71
    single-parent
    below poverty line, 41, 42
    in public housing, 103
Federation of Metropolitan
  Chicago, 164
Foley, Dylan, 131
foster care
  and young male
    homelessness, 48–49
Fox, Cybelle, 69
Funiciello, Theresa, 161

Gallup poll
  on sympathy for homeless, 40
General Accounting Office

on homelessness among
  families and children, 40–41
Germanis, Peter, 53
Gingrich, Newt, 164, 166
Giuliani, Rudolph, 13, 137
  proposals of, to crack down
    on homeless, 138–39,
    143–44
Glaberson, Beatrice, 165
Goffman, Erving, 152
Gore, Tipper, 18
Gospel Rescue Ministries, 160
government
  funding of private charities
    by, 164, 166
  has long supported the needy,
    165–66
  housing subsidies by, 103
  should work to provide
    affordable housing, 91–98
    con, 99–110

Habitat for Humanity, 107,
  108
Haggerty, Rosanne, 127
Hambrick, Ralph S., Jr., 25
Hardman, Peter, 48, 49
Harris, Tim, 147
Health and Human Services,
  U.S. Department of, 16
  on decline in housing
    subsidies, 20
health care
  as barrier to employment, 58
health problems
  among drug-abusing
    homeless, 81
  of homeless adults, 22, 58, 73
  of homeless children, 35–36,
    40
Hess, Robert, 70
Higgs, Suzanne, 121
homeless, the
  average income of, 20

characteristics of, 22, 29, 34, 64–65
criminal behavior among, 26
efforts to criminalize, 143–48
hardcore, should be arrested, 137–41
median age of, 74
mentally ill
  characteristics of, 73–74
  prevalence of, 26–27
  some should be treated involuntarily, 150–54
    con, 155–58
numbers of, 14, 19, 21–22
  among families and children, 40–41
prevalence of substance abuse among, 79–80
private charities can best help, 159–62
    con, 163–67
should not be criminalized, 142–49
homelessness
categories of, 16, 132
causes of, 19–20, 29–30
  are not well understood, 43–44
  domestic violence, 84–87
  lack of affordable housing, 63–67
  low wages and limited employment opportunities, 54–58
  mental illness, 72–77
  substance abuse, 78–83
  unemployment, 47
  welfare cuts, 68–71
  widening gap between rich and poor, 20–21, 37, 56–57
data on, difficulty in obtaining, 42–43
duration of, among families, 41

among employed workers, 29–32, 55–56
is a serious problem for society, 17–22
  con, 23–27
is often voluntary, 25–26, 59–62
among men, 45–50
rural, 33–38
  causes of, 36–38
societal remedies for, 62, 87
  community programs, 148–49
stereotype of, 64–65
stigma of, 18–19
urban, 28–32
among women and children, 39–44
Homelessness, Health, and Human Needs (Institute of Medicine), 27
Homeless Network, 46
homicides
by severely mentally ill, 151
housing
affordable, 20, 37–38
  decrease in supply of, 65–66
  federal government should help provide, 91–98
    con, 99–110
  lack of, as cause of homelessness, 63–67
  and minimum wage levels, 56
policy, should be a local matter, 101–102
public
  costs of, 114–15
  effects of, on homelessness, 146–47
  flaws in, 102, 103–104
  is still being built, 113–14
  redevelopment of, 96–97, 100

Section 8, 95–96, 111
  decline in availability of,
    119–23
  landlord requirements
    under, 123
  waiting period for, 31,
    66–67
  workings of, 124
  vouchers, 95–96
  benefit low-income families,
    111–16
    con, 117–24
  criticism of, 104
Housing and Community
  Development Act (1937), 112
Housing and Urban
  Development (HUD), U.S.
  Department of, 31
  budget proposals for, 94
  establishment and goals of, 90
  housing programs of, 95
    Home Investment
      Partnerships Program, 97
    homelessness and special
      needs, 98
    homeownership, 97–98
    new housing production
      vouchers, 96
    public housing, 96–97
    Section 8 renewals and
      incremental vouchers,
      95–96
  on rental housing, 92–93
  role in addressing housing
    crisis, 94–95
housing ladder
  definition of, 101
  problem with, in housing
    policies, 102
Howd, Aimee, 153
HUD. *See* Housing and Urban
  Development, U.S.
  Department of
Husock, Howard, 99

Hutchinson, Arthur Earl, 145

income
  average
    among homeless, 20
    among mentally ill
      homeless, 73
  gap between rich and poor in,
    20–21, 37, 56–57

Johnson, Gary T., 25
Johnson, Lyndon B., 90

Kaplan, Seymour, 151
Katz, Michael, 165, 167
Klug, Bob, 59
Koegel, Paul, 26
Krauthammer, Charles, 27

Labor, U.S. Department of
  on wage gap, 57
Landaverde, Jose, 148
Landskroner, Jan, 122
Lazio, Rick, 100
legislation
  anti-homeless, 12–13, 30–31
    in Atlanta, 145
    in Chicago, 144–45
    in New York, 143–44
    in San Francisco, 144,
      147–48
    in Seattle, 146
    in Tucson, 146
Lewit, Eugene M., 39
Lydersen, Karl, 142

MacDonald, Heather, 140
Mangano, Philip, 69
Martin, Chance, 155
Matthews, Merrill, Jr., 111
Mbionwu, Elaine Sutton, 157
McKinney Act of 1987, 67
McKinney Homelessness
  Assistance Act of 1987, 90

media
  exaggerates homelessness
    problem, 24–25
  inattention to homelessness
    problem by, 21
men
  are reluctant to seek help,
    49–50
  homelessness among, 45–50
mental illness
  contributes to homelessness,
    72–77
  involuntary treatment of,
    150–54
    argument against, 155–58
  prevalence of, among
    homeless, 26–27
Miller, Leslie, 68
minimal rehab housing model,
  106–107
Mitchell, Pam, 119
Molloy, Aimee, 54
Mulligan, John, 48

National Association for the
  Care and Resettlement of
  Offenders, 47
National Coalition for the
  Homeless, 36, 69, 84, 149
  on homeless population, 16
  on minimum wage levels and
    housing affordability, 56
National Congress for
  Community Economic
  Development, 105
National Housing Act of 1937,
  100
National Institute of Mental
  Health, 77
National People's Action, 149
Nation in Denial, A (Baum and
  Burnes), 79
Nehemiah Plan Homes,
  107–108

Neighborhood Entrepreneurs
  Program, 127
New York Times (newspaper),
  21

O'Hanlon, Ann, 117
opinion polls
  on sympathy for homeless, 40
"Out of Sight—Out of Mind"
  (National Law Center on
  Homelessness & Poverty),
  30–31

panhandling
  restrictions on, 12–13
Pantaleo, Marjorie Kennedy,
  123
People's Weekly World
  (newspaper), 63
Pimenthal, Peggy, 119
Pleace, Nicholas, 49
poverty level, 41
  among children, 37
  and current minimum wage,
    55–56
prison
  release from, and male
    homelessness, 47–48
probation
  assistance for offenders on, 47
psychiatric hospitals. *See*
  deinstitutionalization

Rees, Phillip, 101
*Rental Housing Assistance—The
  Worsening Crisis* (HUD), 92
Roman, Nan, 20
Roosevelt, Franklin D., 53
Rossi, Peter H., 26
Rude Awakenings (White), 24

Safety Network (newsletter), 14
San Diego Regional Task
  Force on the Homeless, 78

Schell, Paul, 146
Scherer, Ron, 127
Seter, Jennifer, 163
Shapiro, Joseph P., 163
Sharpton, Al, 138
shelters
  for abused women, and
    homelessness, 43–44
  availability of, based on
    gender, 46–47
  costs of, vs. SROs, 126–27
  hardcore homeless do not
    want, 139–41
  increase in demand for, 30
  lack of
    for battered women and
      children, 85
    in rural areas, 34
    for substance abusers, 82
  linkage to work, 140
Singer Transitional Residence,
  164–65
single-room occupancy (SRO)
  housing
  conditions in, 130–31
  costs of, vs. shelter housing,
    126–27
  decrease in supply of, 66
  for mentally ill, 76
  as model of private housing,
    105–106
  offers solution to
    homelessness, 125–28
    con, 129–33
  threats to, 132–33
Sobel, Carol, 14
SROs. See single-room
  occupancy housing
Starks, Ernette, 120
"Status Report on Hunger and
  Homelessness in American
  Cities" (U.S. Conference of
  Mayors), 29
substance abuse

has greater impact on
  homeless, 82
is an individual choice, 26
among mentally ill homeless,
  77
prevalence of, among
  homeless, 79–81
suburbs
  expansion of, and rural
    homelessness, 37–38
  households with worst case
    need in, 93
  new housing models for,
    108–109

Tanner, Michael, 159
Temporary Assistance to
  Needy Families (TANF), 53
Terwilliger, Bruce, 123
Tharp, Mike, 13
Thomas, Dave, 118
Thresholds, 148
Tomlinson, Kate, 47
Torrey, E. Fuller, 26, 75, 150
transportation
  as barrier to employment, 57
Tyranny of Kindness (Funiciello),
  161
Tyschenko, Jane, 86

unemployment
  as cause of homelessness
    among men, 47
  homeless parents' reasons for,
    56
United Nations
  definitions of homelessness
    by, 132
Urban Institute
  on homeless population, 14,
    16, 24
U.S. Conference of Mayors,
  29, 66, 69

Van Biema, David, 166
veterans, 48
violence. *See* domestic violence
Vissing, Yvonne M., 33

wages
  inadequacy of, 31
  see also income
Warner, David, 48
Washington Post (newspaper),
  120
Washington Spectator
  (newsletter), 17
welfare reform, 53, 115

effect of, on homelessness,
  29, 146
has increased homelessness,
  68–71
Wilk, Elliot, 138
Winston, Jelada, 123
*Without Shelter: Homelessness in
  the 1980s* (Rossi), 26
women
  are more likely to seek
    emergency services, 49
  homeless, vulnerability of, 46
  homelessness is a problem
    among, 39–44